KYLE BOOKS

Nick Sandler and Johnny Acton

photography by Peter Cassidy

PRESERVED

CONTENTS

FOREWORD

I've long been a fan of Johnny and Nick's culinary double act, not least because I know they share my passion for "real" food—ideally locally sourced, and in season. It's great to see them combine here on such a worthwhile subject, and make the various alchemies of the preservers' art accessible and enticing.

As a stickler for cooking with the rhythm of the seasons, it may seem paradoxical to advocate processes that allow you, for example, to eat raspberries in December. But in many ways, I see preserving as a celebration, not a denial, of seasonality. I'd rather eat my own raspberry jelly (or Johnny's and Nick's grilled green tomato chutney, see page 169) on Christmas Day, than buy fruit and vegetables flown in from halfway around the world.

For those of us who grow our own vegetables and fruit, and rear our own livestock, home preserving is an essential tool in the box of good smallholder practice. It's a way of making the most of the glut of the harvest—bottling it, either literally or metaphorically, for later consumption. But even if you don't have the time and space for raising your own food, you can still tap into the fine fresh produce of those who do (ideally by buying direct from producers at farmer's markets) and dabble successfully in the art of preserving. The fruits of such labor, apart from being delicious, add immeasurably to the home cook's sense of self-sufficiency—and that's a feeling you can't put a price on.

Preserving is about intelligent home economy. It is a matter of maximizing resources, using know-how both ancient and modern to get the most out of your food. But this doesn't imply parsimony or tight-fistedness. If understood and practised well, preserving techniques will never produce food that seems meager, mean, or bland. Instead they introduce a whole new range of flavors and textures to the cook's repertoire, which are as pleasing and exciting as they are diverse.

This is because the key ingredients and techniques for the principal preserving methods—salt and sugar, vinegar and alcohol, oil and fat, smoke, and even plain air—all have radical transforming effects on the raw ingredients exposed to them.

With the judicious inclusion of herbs, spices, and other aromatics, the range of tastes and effects that can be brought about by home preserving is dazzling—and often delightful.

The result is that techniques that began as fairly crude ways of preventing spoilage and laying down stores have developed into some of the higher culinary arts. And preserved foods that were once staples have become our favorite luxuries.

These days most of us rely on commercial processors for our preserved foods—whether it's jellies or pickles, cured meats, or smoked fish. Yet often the scale of these operations involve compromise on ingredients and corner cutting of technique—the inevitable consequences of industrialized food production. What Nick and Johnny have shown here is that the techniques involved are not difficult to master on a domestic scale—and that the process of learning them is both fun and rewarding. Most importantly, they show that the preserved foods you make at home, with the best ingredients you can lay your hands on, can and will be the finest you ever taste.

As an introduction to the subject, *Preserved* is first rate, full of recipes that are both achievable and delicious. Nick and Johnny evidently had a whale of a time exploring the world of food preserving—and there is every chance that, with their guidance, you will too.

Hugh Fearnley-Whittingstall

WHY PRESERVE?

It may sound grandiose, but in many ways the history of civilization is the story of our progressive mastery of food preservation. After all, to be wild is to eat on the run. Learning to prolong shelf-life enabled our distant ancestors to migrate beyond regions where adequate fresh food was available all year round. Later, the construction of cities was premised on our ability to preserve grains, legumes, and animal products. By freeing us from the previously universal imperative to hunt and gather, preserving permitted specialization, giving birth to the arts and sciences. Later still, preserved foods enabled people to survive long sea journeys and thus to colonize the globe. One day, they may allow us to do the same in Space.

Anyone in any doubt about the centrality of food preservation to the way we live should pay a visit to the local supermarket. Almost all of the ingredients we use in our cooking have gone through some kind of preservation process. Take everything cured, smoked, dried, hung, fermented, candied, canned, bottled, frozen, pasteurized, irradiated, or vacuum-packed from the average shopping basket, and you aren't left with much. Just fresh fruit and vegetables and a few fish and poultry products. And probably not even those, unless you go all-out organic.

So food preserving is important, both culturally and historically. Indeed, our distinctive national tastes almost always reflect the preserving techniques dominant in the relevant bit of the world (Scandinavians, for instance, often have a liking for the taste of ammonia as a consequence of the rather drastic methods used by their forebears to preserve fish). But the question remains, why bother to do it ourselves?

TAKING CONTROL OF YOUR FOOD

There are many reasons why home-preserving is a satisfying and worthwhile undertaking. Among the most topical is a growing awareness of the drawbacks of mass-produced food. Some of these are health related, others concern taste. In terms of the former, many people are understandably worried by the additives employed in large-scale food manufacture. When it comes to quality, the end products are frequently compromised by two entrenched habits of the food giants. The first is the use of short-cuts, as time is money in the business world. "Smoked" meats, for example, are often simply infused with "liquid smoke" rather than being produced according to patient, traditional methods. This inevitably has a deleterious effect on taste. The second problem with supermarket food is "averaging"—in other words, catering to the average rather than the individual palate. You may like your kippers smokier or your pickled onions sharper than Mr. and Mrs. 2.4 kids, but if you buy commercial produce, you just have to go with the flow. With home-preserving, you can tailor your food just the way you like it.

Beyond the problems inherent in mass-production, several trends point towards home-preserving. One is the gardening boom. Now that we've taken to growing all these cucumbers and tomatoes, what are we to do when they arrive in sudden gluts? The learning of a few simple preserving techniques opens up a world of possibilities. Then there is the vogue for sophisticated home-cooking. If the transformations that give your ingredients their distinctive character have already taken place by the time you get hold of them (as when you buy a side of smoked salmon), cooking with them will be far less fulfilling than if you prepare them from scratch. With home-preserving, there can be no such problem. The satisfaction goes right to the bottom.

A WORLD OF FLAVOR

Another significant trend is an increasing willingness to experiment with new tastes. In recent years, eating has gone truly global. Home-preserving provides access to a vast range of "foreign" delicacies, many of which are not available in the stores. *Preserved* celebrates this international diversity to the full.

Many other incentives could be added to the list. There is the sheer joy of bringing about amazing and delicious transformations (by concentrating flavors, for example). Then there are the economic benefits—superior preserved foods are much cheaper to make than to buy. They also tend to be aesthetically pleasing, and so make excellent gifts. Plus there is the atavistic thrill of mastering techniques that have been so important to human survival. But above all, preserving is fun.

THE HISTORY AND GEOGRAPHY OF FOOD PRESERVING

Most of the great preserving methods were stumbled upon by accident, too long ago to date with any accuracy. A desperate hunting party found a dead animal lying on a salt-pan, and found that its flesh tasted curiously fresh. A herdsman left a skin of milk in the sun by mistake, later discovering that it had curdled into something rather good. A farmer put some leathery old cabbages in a pot of sea water, forgot about them, and returned to find them shrunken but delicious. But it took acute observation and the sharing of information through language to translate these discoveries into duplicable techniques. Our forebears may not have understood, in our terms at least, why subjecting their food to certain processes kept it wholesome. For them it was a kind of magic, but notice it they did.

CLIMATE AND LOCATION

The particular preserving techniques which took hold in a given part of the world depended on climate and the *modus vivendi* of the inhabitants. Among the nomadic peoples of the deserts and steppes, for whom growing vegetables was clearly not possible, doing clever things with milk was paramount to survival. In the Arctic and in mountainous areas, food froze automatically in winter unless strenuous efforts were made to prevent it. The cool, dry atmosphere of such zones also lent itself to air drying, giving the world such delights as bresaola. In the Mediterranean, Arabia, and parts of the Americas, similar results could be obtained by leaving food in the fierce summer sun, although the products were different, typically consisting of fruits and chiles. Meanwhile, in temperate latitudes where conditions were too moist for effective drying, the accents were on smoking, salting, and pickling. And in Japan, Korea, and other mountainous parts of the Far East, huge populations thrived on fermented legumes and fish, in defiance of the scarcity of cultivable land.

For thousands of years in northern climes, autumn was the cue for a frenzy of preserving activity. Few households owned enough land to provide winter fodder for their livestock, so non-breeding animals were invariably slaughtered before the big freeze. Time was of the essence, and all family members, along with the neighbors, would be enlisted to salt, smoke and dry the flesh, and convert the leftovers into sausages. After the harvest, vegetables, fruits, and fungi all had to be dried or pickled rapidly to prevent them going bad, so their preparation was also a communal undertaking.

In Europe, the pattern went unchanged for generations. The only exception was the arrival of sugar, first introduced in minute and prohibitively expensive quantities by crusaders returning from the Middle East. Its preserving qualities were quickly recognized, but despite the efforts of entrepreneurial farmers in the Canary Islands and elsewhere, it remained beyond most people's budgets until the transformation of the West Indies into one giant sugar plantation during the seventeenth and eighteenth centuries. Suddenly, a whole new range of preserving possibilities opened up to ordinary folk, from jams and marmalades to candied fruits and sugared nuts.

A MORE SCIENTIFIC APPROACH

The greatest revolution in preserving, however, occurred in 1861. In that year, Louis Pasteur published a paper which finally solved the age-old mystery of why food was inclined to go bad. The air, he explained, was teeming with organisms invisible to the naked eye. He had proved this by drawing everyday air through clean guncotton filters and then examining them with a microscope. He had also dropped one of these filters into a sterilized jar of nutritious "soup" and watched the contents start to putrefy. At last people knew the real enemy. Food preserving had previously been an uncomfortably hit-and-miss affair, and the misses had frequently had lethal consequences. But now, with a proper understanding of hygiene and the advent of scientifically sound methods of bottling and canning, safely preserved food became available to the masses. This applied not only to industrially processed products, but also to those made in the home.

We, in our shrunken modern world, are the lucky inheritors of all these techniques. We don't have to live in a desert to eat dried dates or up an Oriental mountain to enjoy a steaming bowl of miso soup. But an appreciation of the rich history behind the many preserved foods that can be successfully made at home can only make them taste better.

DRYING

Where would the Italians be without pasta, or the Chinese without noodles? In serious trouble is the answer. The same could be said of the Egyptians without dried lentils, or even the restaurant-goers of San Francisco without sun-dried tomatoes. Many dried foods are so familiar that it's easy to forget that's what they are.

Prehistoric humans inevitably came across wind-fallen fruits that had dried in the sun. They would have noticed that they didn't look too bad and tasted sweeter and chewier than average, and then that they remained edible for much longer than their fresh equivalents. Any number of forgetful moments around the home would have taught them similar lessons regarding meat.

The systematic removal of moisture from food is the oldest and simplest preserving method of all. It works because potentially contaminating organisms need water to survive. It also concentrates flavor, sometimes to an extreme degree, as in the pungent delicacy euphemistically known as Bombay Duck. Made on the west coast of India by drying small fish in the hot sun, Bombay Duck is intense, salty and almost mineral in texture, but it keeps forever. Herodotus, writing in the fifth century B.C.E., described the Egyptians processing small fish in the same manner. Alexander the Great's troops noticed the residents of Baluchistan in present-day Pakistan making a version of Bombay Duck into flour and even feeding it to their animals.

Their neighbours in Persia and Afghanistan have been adding dried apricots, dates, and mulberries to their stews since time immemorial. Central and South Americans have been air drying strips of meat for just as long. They called the end product *charqui*, which gives us the modern word "jerky." Salt cod was so important historically that the slave trade would arguably have been impossible without it. It was sustained by a triangle in which huge quantities of salted fish were purchased in Newfoundland and New England with commodities from the West Indies, i.e., rum and molasses. This cod was then used to buy slaves in West Africa, and to keep them alive once they had arrived in the Caribbean. The sugar plantation owners paid for the slaves with the products that were in such demand on the North Atlantic seaboard. Thus was the triangle completed, and the traders repeated it indefinitely, taking a substantial profit at every turn. Dried legumes were the chief source of protein in Europe and elsewhere for many centuries, as commemorated in the nursery rhyme: "pease pudding hot, pease pudding cold, pease pudding in the pot nine days old." And dehydrated foods, being light and almost imperishable, have long been vital to armies.

Many of the best dried foods once depended on desiccating mountain breezes or fierce tropical sun, conditions scarcely prevalent in damp corners of the globe like Britain. But with a bit of ingenuity you can now compensate for adverse local conditions. A drying box will prove invaluable. Instructions for building one appear in the recipe for biltong on page 14.

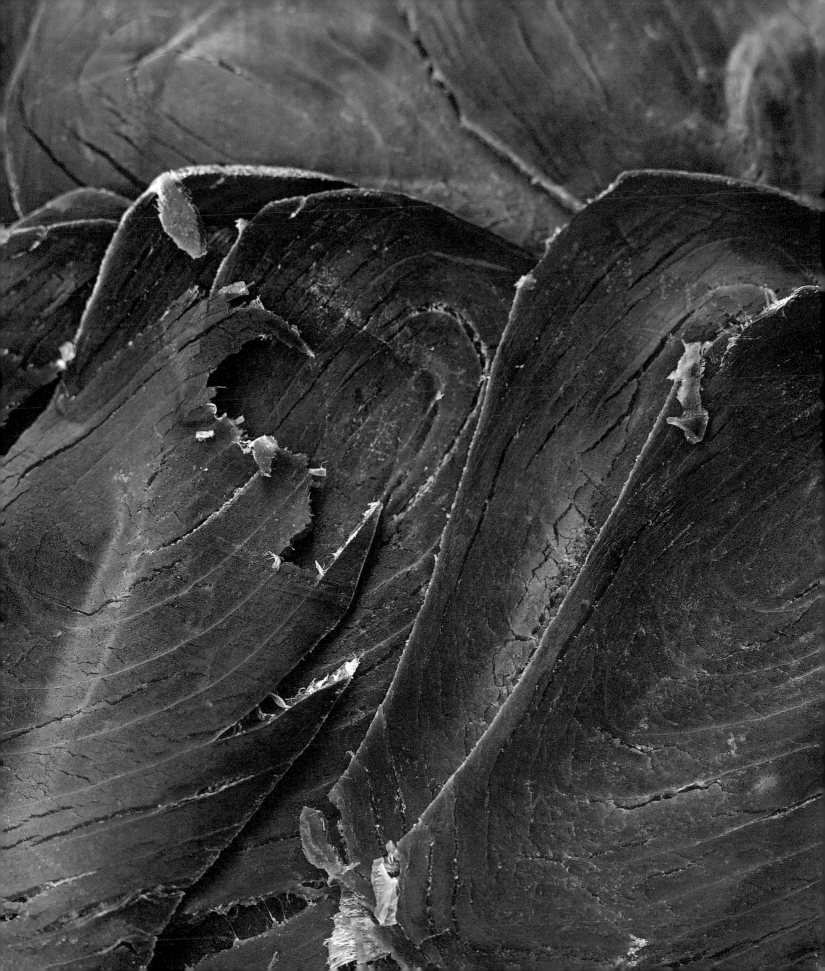

MAKING A DRYING BOX
Use a large wooden or cardboard box (ours is 2½ feet high by 1½ feet deep by 2 feet wide), completely sealed but for a few holes made in the sides towards the bottom and the top. Place a lit 60-watt light bulb inside on the bottom and, to protect it from dripping juices, place a perforated piece of wood or cardboard above the bulb. At the top, secure a rod or length of coat hanger to each side.

BILTONG

Mention biltong to *émigré* Southern Africans and their eyes will start to water with nostalgia. Dark, chewy, and frankly pretty tough, this air-dried, spiced meat is an acquired taste, but once acquired it is never forgotten. Americans already have a head start through their predilection for beef jerky, but never make the mistake of comparing the two in the presence of a South African!

The word "biltong" is of Dutch derivation, "bil" meaning buttocks and "tong" meaning strip, but the Boers learned the technique through contact with the indigenous Bantu. They found biltong an invaluable source of protein during their long wagon trek across the African subcontinent, which began in 1836. The standard spicing is a dramatic blend of vinegar, pepper, salt, sugar, and crushed coriander seeds. These commodities were readily available during the nineteenth century due to the combined efforts of wine-making Huguenot settlers and seafarers stopping off at the colony *en route* from the spice markets of the East.

Biltong can be made from several kinds of lean red meat. Kudu, impala, and ostrich varieties are all popular in its homeland, but the standard form is beef. The difficulty that needs to be overcome is the duplication of the dry atmospheric conditions characteristic of southern Africa. This can be achieved with a measure of success by hanging the strips of meat from a line in a cool, dry place and placing a whirring fan nearby, but if the air is humid, the biltong may still spoil.

A better alternative is to build a drying box. This is remarkably simple (see the instructions to the left), and you can use the box to dry other products—for instance, fruit.

PREPARING THE BEEF

Get a hold of some round steak, or London broil, and cut it along the grain into strips approximately a half-inch thick and six inches long. Cut away any excess fat, as it may otherwise turn rancid. Sprinkle the beef strips liberally with coarse salt on each side and leave them for about an hour. Then scrape off the excess salt with a knife (do NOT use water). Place some cider or wine vinegar in a bowl, and submerge each piece of meat for a second or so before holding it up so the excess drips off. Then sprinkle all over with ground pepper, and coriander seeds.

THE DRYING PROCESS

The meat is now ready to dry. With meathooks or string, suspend the strips towards the top or length of coat-hanger wire which you've secured to the sides. Switch on the light, and leave it on for three to four days, by which time the drying process should be complete. The bulb will produce warm, dry, rising air, and the ventilation holes will help it to circulate.

Variations on the basic theme can be made by painting the meat strips with barbecue, Worcestershire, Tabasco, or soy sauce between the vinegar and pepper/coriander stages.

SERVING AND STORAGE

Biltong is traditionally thinly sliced—in southern Africa they have special machines for the task. Store lightly wrapped in a cool, airy place or refrigerate. Eat within six months.

JERKY

From the American perspective, biltong is the South African version of jerky. For South Africans, jerky is American biltong. The two products do have a lot in common. Both were historically important in the diets of the relevant indigenous populations. They are similarly nutritious and addictive, and ersatz versions of both are increasingly sold and packaged commercially. But they are different enough to make it well worth your while experimenting to decide where you stand in the intercontinental dried meat debate. Jerky is typically made from thinner strips of meat than biltong. Store it in the same way, and eat within six months.

As mentioned in the introduction to this chapter, jerky is a corruption of the word *charqui*. There is some debate about the origin of the term, but the basic technique is continent-wide. The Quechua Incas of Peru cured alpaca meat in salt from local *salares* (salt flats), dried it in the altiplano desert sun, and called it *ch'arki*. In Chile, the guanaco, another relative of the llama, was treated in a similar manner. Chilean miners were among the first on the scene during the California gold rush of 1849. There they took to making jerky from the local cattle and passed on the habit to their fellow prospectors. Meanwhile, the Indians of the North American plains had been drying strips of buffalo meat since ancient times.

TO MAKE JERKY

As with biltong, jerky can be made from almost any lean flesh, including fish. Turkey jerky has a particularly nice ring to it. But the instructions below are for beef jerky, the most popular variety of all.

2 pounds trimmed lean beef (rump is ideal)
1 cup soy sauce
2 tablespoons sugar
3 cloves of garlic
½ medium onion, finely chopped
1 teaspoon Tabasco sauce
2 tablespoons malt vinegar
1 tablespoon Worcestershire sauce
A squeeze of lemon juice

First cut the meat, going along the grain, into strips about a quarter-inch thick.

Next, blend the marinade ingredients until smooth, add the meat, and marinate for six hours minimum in the fridge.

Now you have a choice of drying methods:

SUN/AIR DRYING

Only try this if you live somewhere hot where the air is genuinely arid. Even then, wait for a breezy day. The easiest way to dry your jerky is to hang the strips on a clothesline, protected by some suspended muslin. It is ready when the meat is breakable but not yet brittle; this may take three or four days. But don't use this method for poultry—the risk of spoilage is just too high.

OVEN DRYING

Cover the floor of your oven with tin foil to catch the juices.

Preheat the oven to 180–200°F.

Lay the strips of meat on a wire rack and wipe off the drips. Then "cook" for about four hours with the oven door slightly ajar, turning the meat over halfway though. It may take slightly longer to reach the desired consistency—test it periodically.

SMOKING

If you want to try smoking your jerky, first have a look at chapter Three of this book. Then hot-smoke the jerky for at least two hours (testing it after this period) at about 200°F, or cold-smoke it for longer (6–8 hours at 140°F), finishing it off in the hot-smoker or oven, if necessary.

BRESAOLA

Bresaola is soft, salted and air-dried beef eaten raw. The original and best examples hail from the Valtellina mountains on the borders of Italy and Switzerland. Cut into thin, succulent, almost translucent, ruby-red slices and served with olive oil, lemon juice, and Parmesan, bresaola is one of the classic Italian appetizers.

TO MAKE BRESAOLA
1 large lean rump (around 4½ lbs.) tied tight with string
2 cups red wine (e.g., Chianti)
2 teaspoons ground red chili powder
4 cloves of garlic, crushed
6 bay leaves, shredded
1 lb., 10 oz. coarse salt, e.g., kosher salt
1 tablespoon coarsely ground black pepper
10 sprigs of rosemary, roughly chopped
10 sprigs of thyme, roughly chopped
3 tablespoons sugar
Enough cheesecloth to wrap the beef
Red wine vinegar, for washing

Place the beef in a large tupperware container and cover it with all the ingredients except the cheesecloth and vinegar. Massage them well into the beef. Leave the meat marinate in the fridge for one week, turning it over every day to ensure an even distribution of marinade.

After this period, brush the marinade off the beef and wrap it in cheesecloth. Hang it in a dry, cool place for one month. It will drip for a day or two, so be sure to protect your floor.

The bresaola has matured when it feels firm to the touch. Once it is ready, wash it down with red wine vinegar, then dry it with a cloth. Store in the fridge, preferably in a container, for up to one month.

individual mushrooms will dry faster than others, so you will want to remove them as they reach the desired state. This is when they are crispy to the touch.

STORAGE AND USAGE

The quicker you process your mushrooms after picking, the better the results will be. Dried fungi look great in jars, but make sure they are airtight and kept out of direct sunlight. They will keep for up to eighteen months.

Some soups and stews call for intact dried mushrooms. These will usually need to be soaked beforehand, in which case incorporate the soaking liquid in your recipe as it will have absorbed some of the flavors. Dried mushrooms can also be blended into powder. Use in soups, sauces, and gravies.

DRIED PORCINI AND GRUYERE TARTS

Nick tends to use his best dried porcini for this tart, but it could be made with nutty morels or dried fairy ring champignons. Sometimes, he sets such tarts in his hot smoker (see Chapter Three). **Serves 4**

THE PIE SHELL
1⅔ cups all-purpose flour
½ teaspoon salt
1 teaspoon sugar
½ cup (1 stick) unsalted
   butter, cut into small
   pieces

THE FILLING
2½ cups mushrooms
   (e.g., cremino—small
   portobellos), sliced
¼ cup (½ stick) unsalted
   butter
1 ounce dried porcini
   mushrooms (see page
   21), dirt free, cut into
   small pieces
2 shallots, sliced
   (if unavailable, use 1
   small mild onion)
1 head of garlic, roasted
   as per page 127
¼ cup dry sherry
½ cup crème fraîche
   (if unavailable, use sour
   cream)
1 cup Gruyère cheese,
   grated (if unavailable,
   use Swiss cheese)
5 medium eggs
Paprika
Salt and pepper

- To make the pastry dough, sift all the dry ingredients into a bowl and then, using the tips of your fingers, rub the butter into the flour until it is granular and airy. Add water until the ingredients press together into firm dough. Cover with plastic wrap and leave it in the fridge until you need to roll it out.
- Preheat the oven to 350°F. Roll out the pastry and transfer to a 8- to 10-inch pie dish. Press the pastry dough into the dish, and fold the overlap over the edges so that it hangs down.
- Prick the pie shell with a fork, line it with baking paper or foil, and weigh it down with dried beans or rice.

- Bake for 15 minutes, then remove the paper, and the beans or rice. Increase the heat to 375°F, and bake the pie shell for an additional 15 minutes until lightly colored. Cut off the overlapping crust with a sharp knife.
- To make the filling, fry the fresh mushrooms in the butter over medium heat, with the dried porcini, shallots, and roasted garlic, for a few minutes. Add the sherry, and heat until it has almost evaporated.
- In a suitable bowl, thoroughly mix the crème fraîche, Gruyère, eggs, a little salt and pepper, and the mushrooms.
- Scoop the mixture into the pie shell and sprinkle with paprika. Bake in the oven for 30–40 minutes at 350° until set. Or hot-smoke for one hour at 212°F.

DRIED CHILES

In New Mexico, chiles are treated with the same reverence as wine is among French connoisseurs. The relative merits of different varieties are debated with ferocious passion. Spiky wreaths or ropes of dried chiles called *ristras* hang everywhere. Aside from providing readily available handfuls of the local staple, they also look extremely festive. In recent years, Northern Europeans have cottoned onto this in a big way. In chic boutiques, Christmas trees are now just as likely to be adorned with deep-burgundy dried chiles as they are with more traditional baubles.

Most kinds of chiles can be successfully dried at home, with the exception of thick-walled, meaty varieties like jalapeños. Jalapeños are, nonetheless, excellent when smoke-dried, whereupon they become chipotles (see instructions opposite).

For other species, you will get the best results if you stick to fully ripened chiles, in other words, red ones. Your chiles are fully dried when they snap rather than just bend. They will remain in good condition for up to a year.

RACK DRYING

The easiest and most effective way of rack-drying chiles is to use a food dehydrator, and we strongly advise you to invest in one if you are catching the drying bug (see page 218 for suppliers). The next best approach is to use a home-made drying box, which we showed you how to make on page 14. The third option is to use an oven turned to its lowest setting and with the door left slightly open. This is not particularly economical and may annoy your significant others if they want to cook something else, but at least you don't need any specialty equipment.

If you are using a dehydrator, simply follow the instructions. With the other two methods, it is first advisable to cut the chiles in half lengthwise and remove the seeds (and then watch what you do with your hands for a while!). For oven drying, you should aim for a temperature of 140–160°F and expect to wait 24 hours or more. The drying-box technique will probably take twice as long, but it's less disruptive to your domestic routine.

STRING DRYING/RISTRAS

The easiest approach is to pass a threaded needle through the bottoms of the stems of a succession of chiles until you have a long line of them. But if you are feeling creative, you may want to construct a fully fledged *ristra*. This involves tying chiles together in clusters of three and braiding them along a length of wire. New Mexico chiles are the optimum variety to use. Here's how to go about it:

1) To make a 18-inch *ristra* you will need about seven to eight pounds of fresh chile pods and several five-foot lengths of cotton string.

2) Take three chiles and hold them together by their stems. Wrap the string around the stems twice, then pass it down and then up again between two of the chiles and pull tight so it cuts into the stems slightly.

3) Loop the string around the hand holding the stems, then move the loop so that it rests over the ends of the stems. The free end should hang down through the loop. Pull tightly. Scout guides and sailors will recognize that they have just tied a half-hitch.

4) Continue making clusters every three inches along the string. Continue until all the chiles have been used, starting new strings as necessary.

5) Suspend a length of wire or a straightened coat hanger from a nail, door knob, or other convenient place. Make a small loop at the bottom to prevent the chile clusters from slipping off.

6) Starting with the first cluster of chiles on the end of one of your strings, braid them around the wire, starting at its bottom. Doing this is not unlike braiding a person's hair: the wire serves as one strand and two of the chiles in each cluster act as the other two. First twist one of chiles around the wire, then do the same with another one. Then move on to the next cluster and so on. When you finish braiding one string of chiles, move on to the next one until the *ristra* is finished. Make sure you vary the direction in which the braided chiles point out from the wire to guarantee a nicely three-dimensional *ristra*. And as you finish braiding each cluster, push it down in the center to ensure that the chiles are densely packed.

Whether you've made a simple string or a complicated *ristra*, the next stage is drying. If you are lucky enough to live in a desert region, you can hang your strings of chiles in the sun and wait for them to dry, though bring them in at night to avoid dew. Otherwise, you will need to use one of the techniques listed in the rack-drying section above. Remember to ruffle the chiles up and turn them from time to time to ensure even drying.

CHIPOTLE

Chipotle is the Mexican name for smoke-dried jalapeño. They are easy to make in the hot-smoker, particularly once you've read and digested our smoking chapter.

Take 40 red jalapeño chiles, cutting a lateral slit in each one. Lay them on a rack in the hot smoker and smoke for three to four hours at 212°F. At this point they will be somewhat dehydrated but not completely desiccated. Finish them off in a cool oven (180–200°F) until dry. Chipotles impart a wonderful smoky flavor to stews and sauces and are the key ingredient in adobo seasoning (see page 130).

TOMATOES

In recent times, sun- and semi-dried tomatoes have become indispensible to cooks wherever they happen to live. But unless you can reliably predict several days of breezy weather with low humidity and daytime temperatures in excess of 90°F, which is rarely where we live, you'll have to fall back on other methods. As usual, the chief options are using a dehydrator, a low oven with the door ajar, or your homemade drying box. An ingenious alternative is to place a rack of tomatoes on the shelf under your car's rear window on a hot day.

FULLY DRIED TOMATOES

Drying times will vary according to the size of your tomatoes, but as a rule of thumb, 15 hours in a low oven or 30 in a drying box is about right. However, tomatoes in any given batch will not dry at exactly the same rate, so you need to remove them individually as they become ready. This is when they are firm but no longer juicy.

Whichever method you use, you have two main choices. The first is to cut the tomatoes in half and lay them face up on a fine-meshed rack, sprinkling a few grains of sea salt or kosher salt on each face. The second is to dry them intact on the vine. This involves lying the tomatoes on a similar rack, vine stalk down, before cutting a small cross on the top of each and filling it with a pinch of salt.

Once dried, tomatoes can be stored at ambient temperatures in sealable containers for up to six months. Before use, they will need to be rehydrated by soaking in warm water for half an hour. Dried tomatoes should always be cooked before they are eaten.

SEMI-DRIED TOMATOES

As the name suggests, semi-dried tomatoes are removed from the source of heat halfway through the drying process. They are then packed into sterilized containers (see page 164) which are filled with olive oil. These will keep in the fridge for up to six months. They are moist and more than good enough to incorporate in stews, sandwiches, and sauces without further ado. We've achieved our best results using various varieties of cherry tomatoes.

PISSALADIERE WITH SEMI-DRIED TOMATOES

Pissaladière is the Provençal version of pizza. Whereas the Italians tend to use concentrated tomato sauce as the base flavoring, in the south of France they are as likely to use slices of onion slow-cooked in olive oil. This recipe, which incorporates semi-dried tomatoes, gives you the best of both worlds. At the market in St. Tropez, many kinds of pissaladière are on sale, topped with various permutations of zucchini, goat cheese, pine nuts, and red peppers. **Serves 2–3**

THE DOUGH
3⅓ cups "00" grade flour
2 teaspoons salt
1 teaspoon dried yeast
2 tablespoons olive oil
1¼ cups water, hand-hot

THE TOPPING
2 pounds onions, sliced
  (about 7–8 cups)
½ cup olive oil
A few small sprigs of fresh
  rosemary and thyme or a
  pinch or two of dried
15 anchovies, if salted (see
  page 45), soak before
  use; if preserved in oil,
  they are ready to use
15–20 small black olives
20–30 semi-dried cherry
  tomato halves
  (see page 28)
4 ounces crumbly goat
  cheese—about 1 cup
  (optional)

- First, make the dough. Doing this by hand is fun but you could just as easily throw it together in a food processor.
- Begin by sifting the flour into a large bowl. Mix in the salt and dried yeast, then stir in the olive oil and water with a large spoon.
- Turn the sticky mass out onto a floured surface and knead until it becomes smooth. Or do what you need to get the same result from a food processor.
- Return the dough to the bowl, cover with a damp cloth, and leave in a warm place. Wait for an hour for the dough to rise.
- When this happens, knead it for a minute, then divide it into two balls. You will need just one of them for the pissaladière. The other one can go in the freezer.
- To make the topping, first sweat the onions in the olive oil for 30–40 minutes, along with the rosemary and thyme. Stir frequently and keep the heat low. At the end, the onions should be soft and sweet, but not browned.

- Preheat the oven to 450°F. Roll out the pizza dough gradually, using a little flour to prevent it from sticking. Nick rolls his directly onto a rectangular baking sheet that slots straight into his oven. Alternatively, you could use a pizza stone or rectangular baking tray, or place the pissaladière naked on the shelf of a wood-burning oven.
- Before adding the topping, turn up the edges of the dough by pinching them between your thumb and forefinger.
- Now spread the onion mixture evenly over the dough. Arrange the anchovies in a lattice and sprinkle with the olives, tomatoes, and goat cheese, if using.
- Place in the hottest part of the oven and cook for around 20 minutes. Check after 15 minutes, because ovens are variable in their accuracy. Consume immediately.

FRUIT

When you dry fruit, the flavors intensify and the natural sugars become more concentrated, so it makes sense to use perfectly ripe specimens. Sun drying is great if you can be confident of four or five days of hot, sunny weather, but many of us are seldom that lucky. Otherwise, the best drying vehicle is a multi-tiered dehydrator, though as usual a very low electric oven will do fine, as will a drying box (see page 14). As far as racks are concerned, you can either use the regular wire kind, or weave your own from willow switches. For smaller fruit, you may want to cover your rack with scalded cheesecloth—the scalding is important to keep the material from scorching or passing on its taste to the fruit.

The key to successful drying is that the process should be slow and steady. Too rapid and the fruit will become tough and wrinkled and may split. Too slow and it may rot. It is essential that every fruit in a batch is properly dried before storage. If one remains moist and goes bad, the trouble will spread to all the others. Your fruit is ready when it feels leathery and releases no moisture when squeezed.

Dried fruits can be eaten as they are or else they can be reconstituted by soaking them in lukewarm water or wine for about 24 hours.

SOFT FRUIT

Because of their high water content, soft fruits take longer to dry than hard ones. It is important to keep the temperature below 160°F, at least for the first hour, to prevent the surfaces from hardening, as this would hinder evaporation.

Plums and Damsons

Dried plums are, of course, prunes. Don't let painful memories of school desserts put you off—home-prepared prunes are in another league entirely.

You can slice your plums before drying them, cut them in half, or cut slits in them and remove the pits. Whole plums take longer to dry, perhaps as much as two or three days. Slices should be ready in 12 to 24 hours. We sometimes add a little sugar before drying, but this isn't necessary. We just like 'em sweet.

Smoked prunes are also very good. Hot-smoke them for 12 hours at 212°F, preferably using cherry, apple, or plum wood, and finish them off in the oven at its lowest setting.

Damson plums, which are wild relatives of the plum, can be dried in the same manner as their domesticated cousins.

Nectarines and Peaches

Treat these in the same way as plums, although they are less appealing when smoked.

Figs

Slice and sprinkle lightly with sugar, then dry as per peaches.

Grapes

Use seedless red or black varieties. Blanch in boiling water for a few seconds, then refresh under cold water to help break up the skin and thus speed up the dehydration process. Lay the grapes out on a very fine-meshed rack, otherwise they will fall through. They take rather a long time to dry, about 48 hours in a low oven (176°F), but you can't beat homemade currants and raisins.

Blueberries and Cranberries

Use the same method for blueberries as for grapes. Ditto with cranberries, although we like to dip them in a solution of one tablespoon of honey for every cup of water before drying them, to counteract their tartness.

Bananas

Cut your 'nanas into slices approximately a half-inch thick and soak them in a solution of 30 percent lemon juice and 70 percent water for three minutes. The citric acid in the lemon juice will prevent later discoloration. They will be nice and crispy after about 20 hours in a low oven (176°F).

Strawberries

Slice them about a quarter-inch thick and lay out in a single layer on a drying rack. Turn over once during drying, which should take about 12 hours.

Kiwi Fruit

Simply cut kiwis into slices and dry for around 12 hours.

Pineapples

As per kiwi fruit, only they take longer to dry.

Cherries

These need to be pitted before drying and placed in a single layer on a fine-meshed rack. They will be ready in 18–24 hours.

HARD FRUIT

Dried hard fruits make excellent snacks and are useful as supplements for homemade granola.

Apples and Pears

To make crunchy rings of apple or pear, you first core the fruit with a fruit corer. Then you decide whether you want to skin them or not (we tend to leave the skins on). If you do want them skinned, now is the time. Next, slice them into circles about a quarter-inch thick and dip these for three minutes in a solution made up of a half-cup lemon juice to one cup water to one teaspoon sugar. Then dry the rings in a dehydrator, low oven, or even a microwave, or over a warm radiator. This should take 12–18 hours if you're using an oven. A single layer of apple or pear rings can be dried in three to five minutes in a microwave set to "defrost."

DRIED FIG AND PRUNE MILLE-FEUILLE

If you make this luxurious creamy dessert once autumn has set in, you'll be glad you bothered to make the effort to dry all those figs and plums at the end of the summer. You can either buy the *langue de chat* ("cat's tongue") cookies in the grocery store, or better still make them yourself. **Serves 4**

THE LANGUES DE CHAT
½ cup (1 stick) butter
¾ cup confectioners' sugar
2 medium eggs, lightly
 beaten
1 cup all-purpose flour

THE PRUNE FILLING
¾ cup pitted prunes
1¼ cups port
2 tablespoons sugar

40 dried fig slices (see
 page 32)
1 cup thick cream

- To make the *langues de chat*, preheat the oven to 375°F.
- Cream the butter and confectioners' sugar together and beat for a good few minutes until pale.
- Slowly add the eggs and flour, beating constantly.
- Pipe short lines of the mixture, about two and a half inches long, onto a greased baking tray. Place in the oven and bake for eight minutes, or until slightly colored. Let cool and transfer into an airtight container. This can all be done well ahead of making the mille-feuille.
- To make the prune filling, simmer the prunes in a pan with the port and the sugar until the volume has reduced by at least half. Blend the mixture in a food processor until smooth, and set aside.

- To construct each serving, do as follows: place two *langues de chat* side by side on a dessert plate. Spread a layer of prune purée and cream over the cookies. Then add a layer of dried fig. Then another layer of puree and cream, and finally some more *langues de chat*. Scatter dried fig slices around the plate, and serve with cream or custard. Alternatively, make up some Chantilly cream by adding two tablespoons of sugar and a half teaspoon of vanilla extract (or the seeds from half a vanilla pod) to one cup whipping cream. Whisk until soft peaks form.

SEA BASS WITH DRIED DAMSONS

One satisfying and often very successful way to devise a "new" dish is to take a foreign classic and adapt it to suit local ingredients. Sea Bass with Dried Damsons is a case in point. In China, this would be made with pickled plums. These have a startlingly intense flavor, but some Westerners find them unbearably sour. This is a pity, because the underlying taste combination is a winner. The solution turns out to be to use dried damsons. These wild relatives of the plum are every bit as sharp and flavorful as their Oriental equivalents, but sweeter. And round where we come from, they're pretty much free, since they grow wild. **Serves 2**

10 dried damson plums (see page 32) or use 3 pickled plums
1 sea bass (about 1¼–1¾ pounds), trimmed, scaled and gutted
3 scallions, sliced
2 teaspoons chopped ginger
3 medium-strength dried red chiles (see page 26)

Juice of ½ a lime
Splash of soy sauce
Generous splash of fish sauce
1 teaspoon chopped garlic
1 teaspoon sesame seeds
2 tablespoons sesame oil
1 tablespoon vegetable oil

- Immerse the plums in enough boiling water to cover. Soak for one hour, then remove the pits, and roughly chop the flesh.
- Place the sea bass on the largest flat plate that you can fit in your steamer. If you have to chop the head off, so be it.
- Sprinkle all the remaining ingredients over the fish with the exception of one tablespoon of the sesame oil and the vegetable oil.
- Steam the fish for 12–15 minutes. Sea bass doesn't need much cooking. Gently pierce the flesh through to the bone to see whether it is done. A clear, dark amber sauce will have collected on the plate.
- To finish this dish, heat the remaining oils in a pan until almost smoking, then pour over the fish, which will fizz up dramatically.
- Serve with plain rice, and greens with with oyster sauce.

VENISON WITH DRIED CRANBERRIES

The foundation of this dish is the beef demi-glace which can be frozen successfully, so don't worry if you make too much. The cranberries are added right at the end. **Serves 4**

THE DEMI-GLACE

4 pounds beef bones, cut
 into small pieces
1 pound veal bones, cut
 into small pieces
4 cloves of garlic
2 carrots
½ cup fresh mushrooms
1 large onion, cut in half
3 stalks of celery
1 medium leek (about
 4 ounces)
½ cup wheat flour
A sprig of thyme
6 tablespoons tomato
 paste

A sprig of parsley
A sprig of rosemary
4 bay leaves
⅓ ounce dried porcini
 mushrooms (see page 21)
½ teaspoon peppercorns
salt
½ cup port

THE MAIN DISH

½ cup dried cranberries
 (see page 32)
1 pound venison strip loin
Salt and pepper
A little olive oil
Fresh dill, for garnishing

- To make the demi-glace, preheat the oven to 400°F and roast the beef bones, veal bones, garlic, carrot, fresh mushrooms, onion, celery, and leek in an oven dish for one hour or until lightly browned. Sprinkle the flour on top and roast for another 10 minutes.
- Transfer the contents to a large pot and swish out the bottom of the oven dish with boiling water. Scrape off the juicy bits and pour them into the pot. Add the thyme, tomato paste, parsley, rosemary, bay leaf, porcini, and peppercorns.
- Top up with water to around one and a half inches above the bones and bring to a boil. Simmer for at least eight hours. Regularly skim the surface of the demi-glace for fat and impurities.
- Strain the demi-glace through a conical bouillon strainer into a clean pan. Reduce to around one and a half quarts by boiling gently, and season with salt.
- Scoop out two cupsful of the demi-glace and freeze for another use.
- In another saucepan, heat the port until reduced. Then add the remaining four cups of the demi-glace, along with half the cranberries, and simmer for 40 minutes. Strain through a conical bouillon strainer or cheesecloth-lined collander, pressing the cranberries firmly as you do so to smash them. Then add the remaining of the cranberries to the collected juice, and simmer while you cook the venison.
- Season the venison and dab the meat with a little olive oil. Sear in a frying pan on each side, then place over very low heat and continue to cook until rare, medium, or however else you like it.
- Spoon a little demi-glace onto each plate with a few cranberries, and then lay slices of venison on top. Garnish with the fresh dill, and serve.

FRUIT LEATHER

Fruit leather is essentially concentrated fruit, puréed, dried, and rolled into sheets. The colors are vivid and the flavors intense. Kids love fruit leather and you have the comfort of knowing they are snacking on something healthy.

You can have fun experimenting with leathers made from a variety of fruits and combinations thereof. We give you recipes for a couple of winning formulas below. The first is lovely and yellow, the second lovely and purple. Just remember to add lemon juice if you are using fruits that are liable to discolor. If you overcook your leather, it becomes brittle and difficult to peel off the silver foil or plastic wrap. The same applies if you add too much honey or sugar.

MANGO AND YELLOW PLUM FRUIT LEATHER
Makes 1 sheet

1 medium mango, ripe and sweet
4 medium yellow plums
½ cup honey

- Peel and dice the mango and do the same with the yellow plums.
- Place the fruit in a saucepan along with the honey, and simmer for five minutes.
- Blend with an immersion blender until smooth.
- Line a medium-sized rectangular baking tray with plastic wrap or foil and pour in the mixture until it just runs to the sides.

- Place in an oven heated to 160°F and leave it for about six hours. The leather is ready when it is tacky but no longer sticky.
- Let the leather cool, then roll it up in plastic wrap or cut it into strips and store them in an airtight container in a cool place. It will keep for two months at ambient temperature in a dark place, four months in the fridge or one year in the freezer.

SALTING

If you are lucky enough to attend a sumo wrestling bout in Japan, you will see enormous men in loincloths cast handfuls of salt over the ring before they charge at each other with the momentum of mini-elephants. The idea is to ward off evil spirits. Salt is associated with purity, and evil spirits can't handle that.

DRY-SALTED ANCHOVIES

SALTED CAPERS

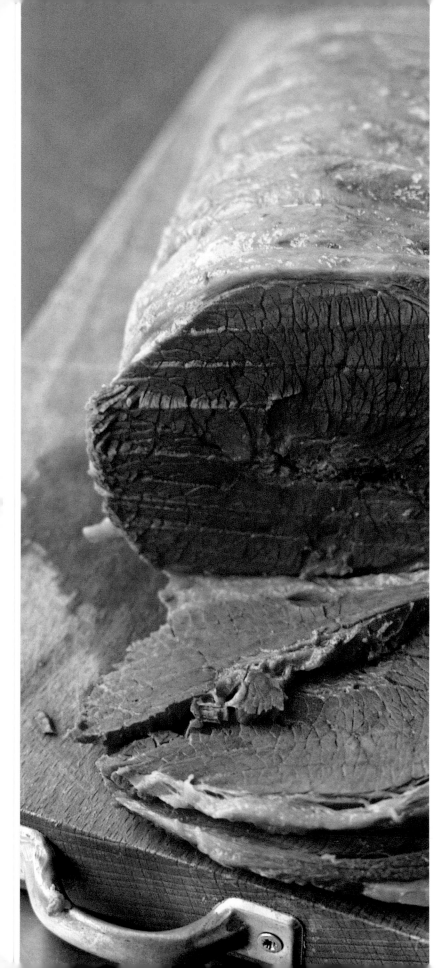

BEEF

The nomenclature of salted beef products is a food editor's nightmare. When Americans refer to "corned beef"—the sliced, not canned variety, they usually mean what the British would call "salt beef," namely whole cuts of cured meat. What Brits and Americans both call "corned beef," is highly processed, canned South American beef. To clarify, we use "salt beef" to refer to the kind of meat used in a reuben sandwich, while "corned beef" is what the Irish, and still more the Irish Americans, traditionally eat with cabbage on St. Patrick's Day.

OLD-FASHIONED CORNED BEEF

The "corn" in corned beef has nothing to do with corn, but instead refers to the nuggets or "corns" of salt traditionally used to preserve the meat. Nowadays, corned beef is usually made with brine rather than dry salt, but the old name lives on. Once cooked, corned beef is fantastically tender.

- 3 cups sea salt or kosher salt
- 3½ quarts fresh water
- 4 cloves of garlic
- 1 large onion, rough chopped
- 2 tablespoons whole mustard seeds
- 2 tablespoons whole coriander seeds
- 1 tablespoon whole cloves
- 3 tablespoons whole peppercorns
- 2 large bay leaves
- 1 tablespoon thyme
- 1 beef brisket, about 5–8 pounds

You need to use a non-metallic vessel for brining. An enamelled churn would be ideal, as would a plastic or polystyrene ice chest.

Mix the sea salt and the water and stir until all the salt is dissolved. The brine is the correct strength when a fresh uncooked egg will float in it. If it doesn't, add a quarter-cup of salt at a time until it does.

When the brine passes the egg test, add the remaining ingredients and the brisket. The meat needs to be submerged at all times, so weigh it down, e.g., with a plate with a large stone on top.

Cover the brining vessel and refrigerate for about 10 days, turning the brisket over every other day. The thicker it is is, the longer it will take to cure. When the beef has finished curing, you can use some of it immediately and refrigerate (for up to two weeks) or freeze the rest for another day (it will keep for six months).

To cook the corned beef on its own, cover it with water, bring it to a boil, skim the surface, and simmer for about four or five hours. It is ready when tender.

To make a traditional Paddy's Day dinner, take about four and a half pounds of corned beef, place it in a pot suitable for long, slow cooking and cover it with water. Add one tablespoon of chopped fresh parsley, one teaspoon of powdered mustard, a couple of bay leaves, four cloves, and about 10 black peppercorns. Bring this to a boil, cover the pot, turn down the heat and simmer for three hours. At the end of this period, skim the fat from the top and pour away half the water. Then add a large head of green cabbage, cut into wedges, and a dozen small, peeled onions. Place the beef on top of these vegetables and simmer on for another half an hour.

SALT BEEF

Although Europeans and Americans have been salting beef for donkey's years, Jewish chefs are the ones who have really got the recipe down pat. This is probably because salt pork, being non-kosher, was never much of an option to members of that faith. They therefore poured all their creative energies into mastering the preserving of beef.

The most interesting ingredient in the recipe that follows is saltpeter, also known as potassium nitrate. Saltpeter has played an important role in military history, partly through being liberally added to soldiers' food to curb their libido, partly as a major constituent of gunpowder. But in this context it has a much more benign effect. As well as allowing the meat to retain its bright pink color when cooked and adding a distinctive and desirable flavor, it also inhibits the growth of harmful bacteria.

Getting hold of saltpeter can be problematic, as people are reluctant to sell it owing to its potential use in the manufacture of explosives. Any Jewish cook worth his salt will have a steady supply, but the rest of us may have better luck finding sodium nitrite (with two 'i's), which is just as effective. If you draw a complete blank, don't worry: the function of these exotic additives is largely cosmetic and you can make excellent salt beef without them.

INGREDIENTS

- 1 heaped tablespoon salt
- 1 heaped tablespoon saltpeter (if obtainable)
- 4½ pounds rolled beef brisket
- 2 quarts beef broth or water
- 1 teaspoon black peppercorns
- 4 bay leaves
- 1 teaspoon salt
- ½ teaspoon caraway seeds
- 2 carrots
- 1 onion, cut in half

Dissolve the salt and saltpeter in a cup of warm water.

Place the meat in a bowl just big enough to contain it and cover with cold water, adding the dissolved salt and saltpeter.

Cover the bowl and leave it in a cool place for three days.

After this period, the water will be tinged pink and the meat itself will be a dull red. Remove the beef and rinse it well.

Simmer the beef in beef broth or water, along with the peppercorns, bay leaves, salt, caraway seeds, carrots, and onion for around three hours until the beef is nice and tender. (You can reuse the broth to make sauce or a classy borscht.)

Let the beef cool in the stock to keep it juicy, then remove it and store it in the fridge for up to a week, or in the freezer for up to six months. Now you can make some sublime sandwiches.

SMOKING

Smoked foods are delicious. Period. Impregnating a fish, fowl or hunk of meat with fragrant hardwood smoke concentrates the flavor and transforms the color and texture. In fact, your authors are hard pressed to think of any of the regularly smoked foods that isn't improved by the process.

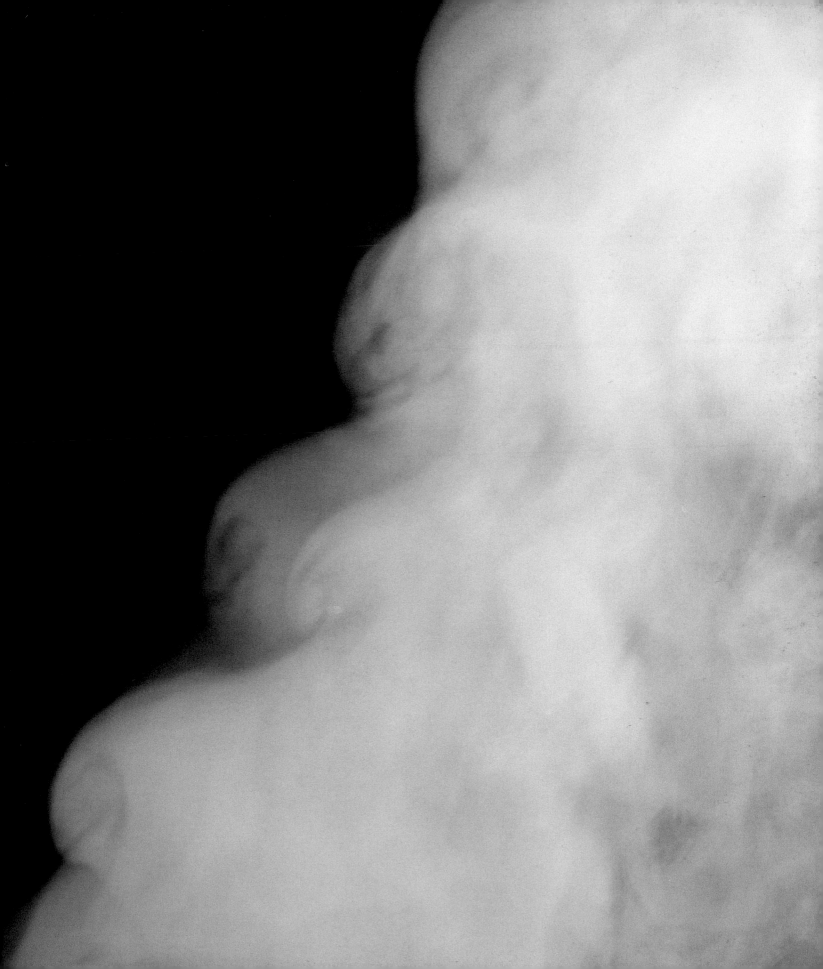

Like most of the techniques in this book, smoking was discovered by accident. At some point in the distant past (and archaeology suggests people have been using fire for at least 400,000 years), someone discovered that pieces of meat left hanging in whatever smoke-filled cave or hovel they were living in at the time remained edible for much longer than might have been expected. They tasted great too. Before long, it also became apparent that smoking food could save lives during times of scarcity.

By the Middle Ages, many northern European farmhouses had special smoking shelves built into their chimneys and in some coastal areas smoking was already established as an industrial process.

THE SCIENTIFIC BIT

The preservative powers of smoke rest on a number of exotic constituents, including antioxidants like butylated hydroxyanisole and various alcohols and phenols. Although the quantities involved are minute, these are not all the healthiest of substances, so it would be unwise to subsist entirely on smoked foods.

As a kind of double insurance policy, most smoked foods are dry-salted or brined for a period prior to the main event. This curing reduces their water content, firms up the flesh, and seasons it. Nowadays, with the advent of freezers and vacuum packs, flavor is relatively more important, and longevity less so than they once were, so smoked foods are typically salted and smoked for shorter periods.

HOT AND COLD SMOKING

The crucial division in home-smoking is between cold and hot. In cold smoking, the temperature in the chamber is not allowed to rise much above that of an ordinary room, drying the food but not cooking it. Typical cold-smoked products include salmon and fillet of beef. If the temperature rises above 85°F while you are smoking them, you should start to worry. Fish, in particular, may start to disintegrate, and microbes to proliferate. Hot smoking, on the other hand, partially cooks the relevant items and usually requires a temperature of between 180°F and 200°F for fish (such as mackerel), and a rather broader range of 180°F) to 240°F for poultry and meat. Beware of the gray zone between these "bandwidths." We'll deal with hot smoking later in the book, but for now we'll concentrate on cold (incidentally, most hot-smoked foods require a preliminary period of cold smoking before stage two).

COLD SMOKING

Cold-smoking doesn't actually cook food, it just flavors it and gives it a long shelf-life. Some cold-smoked products, like smoked salmon, and beef, are best eaten raw. Others, like kippers, you'll want to cook before consumption.

THE SIX STAGES

1) Weighing. The best way to tell whether an item is sufficiently smoked is to weigh it and compare the figure with its initial weight (that is, its initial weight after removing surplus fat but before brining or salting). You should make a note of the original weight or you may forget it. By and large, fish need to lose less weight than cuts of meat, but we'll give you the appropriate percentages for each product with the relevant instructions.

2) Brining or Dry-Salting. This is vital as it removes moisture from the food and renders it unappetizing to bacteria. Brining is sufficient for most smoked products—the only item we've instructed you to dry-salt is bacon, and even this is negotiable.

3) Drying. Whether you've dry-salted or brined your victuals, you'll need to hang them for a period prior to smoking them or they will be too moist to smoke properly.

4) Smoking. The main event. As mentioned in the spiel at the start of this chapter, you need to make sure the temperature inside your cold-smoker never rises above 85°F during the smoking phase.

5) Maturing. After you've finished smoking, the flavorants from the smoke will continue to penetrate the flesh for a while. Most smoked products will benefit from a good 24 hours of maturation before consumption.

6) Storage. Smoked foods will keep in the fridge for at least a week and quite often a good deal longer, but they also freeze well. Wrap them in foil before stashing them in the freezer.

The instructions for smoked salmon, the first cold-smoked delicacy you will come to as you read on, provide a detailed example of the standard sequence in action.

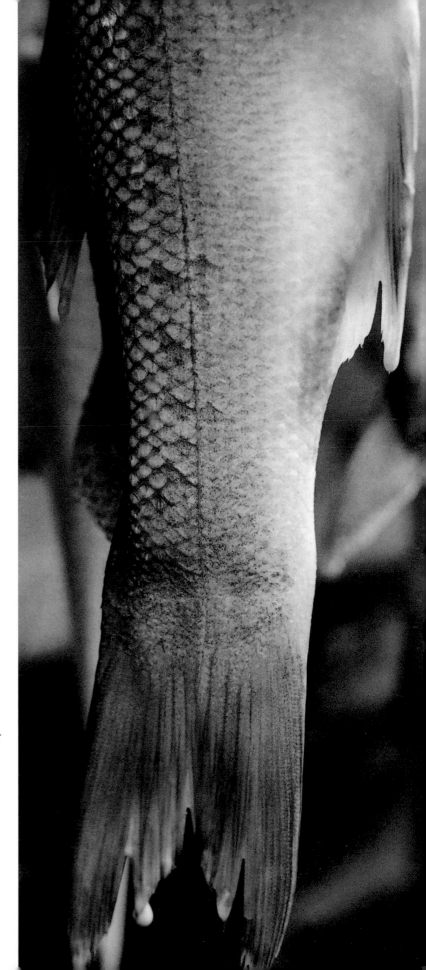

BUILDING A COLD SMOKER

In the simplest terms, what you need is a sufficiently large chamber to allow you to hang or support a decent-sized fish from somewhere near the top with room to spare, and having a ventilation hole or holes near the top of the chamber to act as a chimney, and a hearth or metal plate to house the sawdust, with a perforated piece of wood or metal a few inches above to disperse the smoke evenly as it rises. Once you grasp the principles, there are many ways to skin the cat. Here we'll teach you to build a simple wooden or cinderblock smokehouse from scratch. This is a most satisfying undertaking.

THE TWO ALTERNATIVES

The first consideration is the method of delivering the smoke. The two alternatives are lighting a smouldering fire inside the smoker itself or piping it in from a remote chamber, à la Nick's glorious pictured device. The first approach is only advisable if the smoker is rather large: you don't want the burning material to significantly increase the internal temperature. If you choose the latter method, go to the local home improvement store and buy a length of flexible aluminum tubing four to six inches in diameter, to channel the smoke in the desired direction.

THE SMOKING CHAMBER

Turning to the main chamber, an ideal size for domestic use would be in the order of five feet high by three feet broad and deep. If you use cinderblocks, the construction is child's play. If you prefer to use wood, which is more attractive, but obviously more combustible, make sure it hasn't been treated with anything vile that might taint the food. Buy enough planks to do three sides plus a roof if you'll be building a door, or four sides if you're more inclined towards a lid (see photograph). The chamber will be significantly sturdier if you reinforce each side by nailing three beams to the planks in a "Z" shape.

BUILDING THE FRAME

The first step is to build a frame. You will need four three-foot pieces of wood for the base, four three-foot pieces for the top and four five-foot pieces for the corner posts. The next stage is to nail the planks to the frame, the exact configuration being dependent on your preferred method of access. If you are handy at this sort of thing, you might want to consider installing a door, otherwise a wooden lid (preferably hinged) is perfectly adequate for getting your foodstuffs in and out.

Next, install two battens on the inside of the box, about 18 inches from the ground, to support the smoke diffuser. If you intend to produce your smoke inside the chamber, you'll need another two battens below them to house the metal plate on which your wood will smoulder. Leave enough room underneath for ignition purposes (see next paragraph). If you are planning to rest your fish and meat on racks, you will need a couple of pairs of extra battens higher up in the chamber. If, on the other hand, you plan to hang your food, you can either drill small holes in the sides and pass appropriate metal hanging rails between them, or, following our example, screw some hooks into your hinged lid. If you do this, you want to make sure you can't or don't open it a full 90 or 180 degrees, or the food you are smoking will bang against the lid and any unoccupied hooks.

PRODUCING THE SMOKE

The final piece of the jigsaw is to sort out your smoke source. You will need to make some vent holes a couple of inches below the roof to draw the smoke up and out. If you're going for the remote fire-pit technique, you'll need to cut a hole that is the diameter of your aluminium tubing on one side, near the bottom, and secure it. Otherwise, you'll want to ignite your fuel, probably in the form of sawdust, by placing a small gas burner underneath the metal plate on which the food is to rest. If you leave a gap at

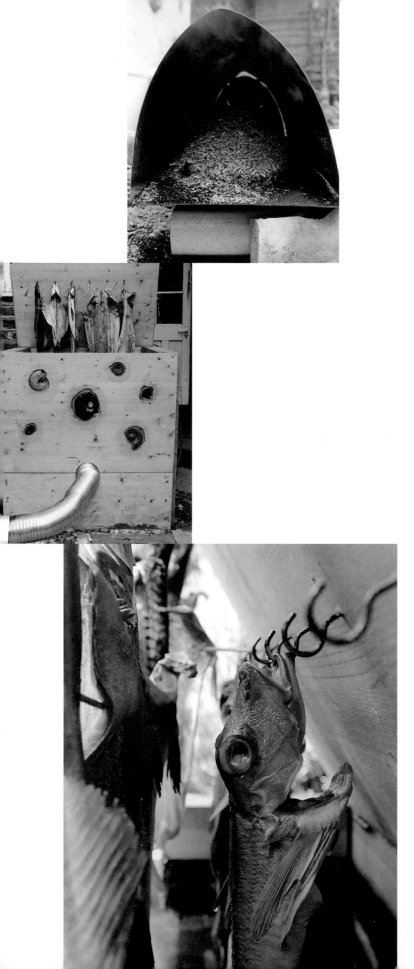

the bottom of the front of the smoker (perhaps by using slightly shorter planks on this side and nailing them to an extra crossbeam a few inches above the bottom), it will make this considerably easier.

Don't be daunted. It's easier than it sounds, and if your smoker leaks in a few unexpected places, it's no big deal. In fact, the hardest part of the process in our experience is finding a reliable source of fuel. By far the most user-friendly material is sawdust. We'd recommend that you purchase a cheap electric planer to make your own. A couple of cookie-tinfuls will smoulder happily for a good 10 hours. The crucial thing is to avoid softwoods such as pine, which will give your food an unpleasant, antiseptic taste. We tend to use oak, but beech, birch, hickory or any fruit wood will do just as well—perhaps better, as they tend to produce more smoke and each imparts a subtle flavor of its own. You should be able to buy hardwood planks from timber merchants.

SAFETY PRECAUTIONS

Igniting your sawdust can be tricky—you don't want it to burst into flame—but you'll soon get the hang of it. Some strategic blowing may come in handy. As mentioned previously, smoke produced in either of the suggested ways is unlikely to heat your chamber to danger level, but you might want to purchase a candy thermometer just to make sure. Above all, refrain from smoking in hot weather. If the outside temperature is above 80°F, you don't have much of a chance. It is no accident that the traditional time of year for smoking is fall.

SMOKED SALMON (LOX)

If you are anything like us, the first thing you'll be itching to smoke is a salmon. The undisputed king of smoked foods, S.S. is often pretty good if you buy it from the store. If you make your own, it can be sublime. You'll also be very popular with your friends. There is one more consideration. Store-bought smoked salmon tends to be four or five times the cost of the fresh equivalent. Why is anyone's guess—making it is virtually free. 'Nuff said.

It would be faintly sacrilegious to smoke a wild salmon unless you found yourself in the Arctic with a mountain of them, because in Britain at least we have hardly any left. But you do want to buy the freshest, firmest farmed fish you can lay your hands on.

SPLITTING/FILLETING

You have a choice between filleting the fish or splitting it. Filleting is the better option in the case of very large salmon or if you plan to lay the fish on a rack during smoking. A seller in a fishmarket will happily do it for you. To split a fish, take a sharp knife and cut the animal down the back from head to tail. Remove the guts, gills, and blood channels, particularly the large one running along the spine, and wash the fish thoroughly.

WEIGHING

Once you have gutted the fish, weigh it. This will allow you to determine, after it's smoked, when it is done. The salmon should diminish in weight by 17–18 percent during the smoking process. In other words, a fish which tips the scales at 12 pounds after gutting should weigh around 9 pounds once smoked.

BRINING

An 80 percent salt solution is about right for this stage. This equates to 2lb., 10 oz. of salt to every 4 1/2 quarts of water. Make sure you use coarse salt such as kosher salt. You will need to weigh down the fish to prevent it floating to the surface. Leave the fish in the brine for one to three hours, depending on its size and fat content (fat salmon will need a longer immersion time than skinny ones).

DRYING

At this stage, you need some string. Use it to suspend the salmon via the tail, or thread it through the eye sockets, or pass the string through incisions made under the shoulder plates. You will also need wooden skewers or small hazel twigs to hold the fish open. These can be easily inserted into the flesh. Hang the fish to drip-dry in the inactive smoker for 24 hours. Don't rinse off the brine.

SMOKING

The desirable duration of smoking depends on three things: a) personal taste, b) ambient temperature, and c) humidity. The colder or more humid the weather, the longer the process. On average, you are looking at anything from 24 hours to two and a half days. The acid test, as mentioned above, is to weigh the fish from time to time, aiming for a 17–18 percent reduction in weight.

MATURING

You should refrain from eating the salmon for a good 24 hours, to allow the smoky surface deposits to work their way inside.

STORAGE

If you keep it in the fridge, your smoked salmon will be in tip-top condition for five days and more than edible for 10. It also freezes well, provided you first wrap it in aluminum foil.

SMOKED SALMON, NOODLES, AND SWEET CHILI SAUCE

This Oriental-inspired dish is an excellent way to use some of your proudly smoked salmon. The mild, sweet chili sauce is slightly gelled and tinged pink. It perfectly complements the amber translucence of the salmon, as do the glassy noodles, and it keeps in the fridge for months. **Serves 2**

4 ounces rice noodles
4 ounces baby greens or shredded spinach (about 2 large handfuls)
Salt
2 teaspoons sesame seeds
2 heaped tablespoons sweet chili sauce (see page 177)
4 ounces smoked salmon, cut into strips (about 1 cup)

- Make the sweet chili sauce following the recipe on page 177.
- Cook the rice noodles as per the instructions on the package, then chill in cold water and drain thoroughly.
- Plunge the greens/spinach in boiling salted water for about a minute, then chill in iced water and drain as above.
- Dry-fry the sesame seeds in a small pan over medium heat until golden (approximately two minutes).
- Throw the noodles, sweet chili sauce, salmon, and baby greens together in a large bowl and mix. If you like, you can heat the salad slightly in the microwave.
- Divide between two plates, scatter the sesame seeds on top, and serve.

SMOKED BACON

This recipe is for pancetta-style bacon made from pork belly. Decent unadulterated bacon is hard to come by in the supermarkets, and although organic bacon is increasingly available, for some reason it is rarely both smoked and from the pork belly. This is difficult for us as we're no great fans of back bacon cuts (like Canadian bacon). "Too little fat!" we cry. Generous seams of fat not only add flavor, they also render down to make an excellent frying medium. For this reason alone, you are better off using pork belly from free-range pigs, which tend to be fatter than their unfortunate fellows from factory farms.

We wouldn't attempt this with less than 22 pounds of pork belly, partly because it will lose up to 30 percent of its pre-salted weight during smoking, partly because it is so good that you may end up proudly giving a lot of it away. A meat-filleting knife will prove invaluable.

TO MAKE PANCETTA

- **9 pounds sea salt or kosher salt**
- **9 pounds sugar**
- **22 pounds pork belly, ribs and gristle removed (your butcher should be happy to remove the ribs and gristle or you can do it yourself with a filleting knife. If you do, buy slightly more pork belly to compensate)**
- **1 large branch of dried rosemary**
- **1 large tupperware or non-reactive container**

Mix the salt and sugar together to make a sweet cure.

Sprinkle a layer of the sweet cure into the bottom of the container, then a layer of pork, then another layer of sweet cure and so on, finishing with a layer of salt. Continue until all the pork is used up and packed hard with the sweet cure.

Leave in a cool place to cure. After two days, pour away any excess liquid and re-pack the pork upside down and in reverse order (i.e., the seam of meat that was at the top should now be at the bottom). If too much of the sweet cure has dissolved, you can top it up with some more.

After three more days, wash the pork off with cold running water, then sprinkle with a little sea salt or kosher salt, and rosemary.

Air-dry in a cool area for 24–48 hours.

Cold smoke for 48 hours at 75–80°F. We pierce the meat and thread string through to hang it from hooks, but you can use racks if you prefer. Wood-wise, oak is great, but cherry, beech, or sweet chestnut are also good.

Your bacon is ready for frying immediately. Nevertheless, we like to let it mature in the fridge for a month, by when it is a deep, almost translucent amber.

The bacon can be stored in the fridge for up to three months, but make sure you keep it dry. Look out for dark molds. If any form, throw the meat away.

Before using this pancetta-style bacon, trim off the skin. You can either slice the bacon very thinly to make breakfast strips of bacon or dice it for use as an ingredient in sauces and stews.

PEA AND SMOKED PANCETTA SOUP

Pulses and bacon products have a natural affinity. Here, the salty tang of pancetta is offset by a naturally sweet petite peas puree. **Serves 4**

5 ounces diced smoked pancetta—about ¾ cup (see page 71)

3 ounces leek, washed and roughly chopped (about 1 cup)

5 ounces onions, roughly chopped (about ⅓ cup)

2 tablespoons butter

5 cups chicken broth

14 ounces potatoes, peeled and diced (about 2½–3 cups)

1 teaspoon salt or more according to taste

¼ teaspoon ground white pepper

¼ teaspoon ground bay leaf or 2 whole ones

18 ounces petite peas (about 4–4½ cups)

A sprig of mint, chopped

⅔ cup heavy cream

- Fry the smoked pancetta over medium heat until nicely browned. Remove the bacon and set aside.
- In the same pan, sweat the leek and onions in the butter and the bacon fat until soft.
- Pour in the chicken broth, then add the potatoes and simmer for 20 minutes.
- Add the salt, pepper, bay leaf, and petite peas, and simmer for another 10 minutes.
- Blend the soup with an immersion blender until smooth. If you are using whole bay leaves, remove them before blending.
- Add the mint, cream, and pancetta, and serve immediately.

SMOKED EGGS

It may never have occurred to you to smoke eggs but now is the time to consider it. It is difficult to say what the process does to their flavor without using the word "smoky," but it makes them a lot tastier and gives them a remarkable color. If you smoke a few when you get up, they will be ready for a late snack.

Don't use newly-laid eggs as they are difficult to peel. Quail eggs are at least as good smoked as hens' eggs and need a lot less time in the smoker.

PREPARING THE EGGS

To smoke either kind of egg, place them in a pan of cold water, bring quickly to a boil, remove from the heat, and leave them in the water to cool. With quail eggs, you need to arrest the cooking process by refreshing them under cold water after 3 minutes.

Peel the eggs before smoking and season them with salt and white pepper and perhaps a little soy sauce. Place them on racks in your smoker and smoke them at about 80°F. Hens' eggs take about 12 hours, quail eggs between four and six. They will keep in the fridge for up to two weeks.

SMOKED HADDOCK AND EGG PIE

Smoked eggs are excellent in salads and sandwiches and go particularly well with smoked haddock in a pie. To make one to feed four people, boil and then mash 6 medium potatoes with one-half cup milk, 3 tablespoons butter, salt, pepper and one cup grated sharp cheddar. Dice 9 ounces smoked haddock (about one cup) and mix it with 6 diced smoked eggs, 1½ cups béchamel sauce, some chopped parsley, and a little grated nutmeg. Spread the potato on the fish mixture and grate some cheddar on top. Bake in the oven for 45 minutes at 400°F. This recipe cries out for peas as an accompaniment.

SMOKED CUSTARD TARTS

This isn't the most obvious recipe on the planet, but try it and you may be pleasantly surprised. **Makes 2**

THE PASTRY DOUGH
    3¾ cups "00" grade all-purpose flour
    1⅓ cups confectioners' sugar
    1 cup plus 2 tablespoons butter (2¼ sticks)
    1 medium egg, plus 2 egg yolks
    ½ teaspoon natural vanilla extract

Sift the flour and sugar into a large bowl. Work in the butter with your fingers until soft and crumbly. Then mix the egg, yolks and vanilla together, make a well in the flour, then stir in the egg until a soft dough is formed.

Loosely roll out the dough and divide it into two balls. Cover in plastic wrap and let rest in the fridge for 30 minutes before using.

Take two eight-inch tart pans with removable bottoms, about one and a half inches deep. Roll out the dough and press it out into the pans, leaving it hanging slightly over the lip. Place a sheet of foil over it, evenly spread some dried beans or legumes and bake blind for 10 minutes in a preheated 360°F oven. Then remove the beans, trim the crust, and cook on for another 15 minutes.

THE CUSTARD
    8 medium eggs
    2¼ cups milk
    2¼ cups heavy cream
    1⅓ cups superfine sugar
    2 teaspoons natural vanilla extract
    Freshly ground nutmeg

Lightly whisk the eggs, and then add the milk, cream, sugar, and vanilla extract and hand-beat for 30 seconds.

Fill the tart shells, then bake in the oven at 300°F for 45 minutes or until the custard has just set. Cold-smoke the tarts for two hours and serve.

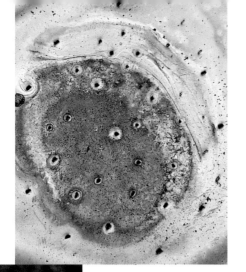

HOT SMOKING

Hot smoking, in contrast to cold, cooks whatever is being smoked. As mentioned previously, hot-smoked products almost always undergo a period of cold smoking beforehand. It is during this phase that most of the moisture loss and the greater part of the smoke flavoring take place.

Hot-smoked fish need to be processed within quite a narrow temperature range, namely between 180–200°F. Any colder and they enter the danger zone for bacterial growth; any hotter and they start to disintegrate. Meats are more tolerant. They can be successfully hot smoked at anything between 180–240°F. Some products, particularly oily fish like mackerel and salmon, are suitable for both kinds of smoking. It is worth experimenting to see which you prefer. Other foods can only be successfully cold smoked—cheese, for instance, will simply melt if placed in a hot smoker. Still others, including poultry and most kinds of game, are only really amenable to hot smoking. It is worth bearing in mind that hot smoking takes much less time than cold.

BUILDING A HOT SMOKER

The simplest way to build a hot smoker, and the one we would recommend, is to adapt a galvanized garbage can or trash-incinerator. All you need to do is punch several holes in the bottom of the garbage can, perhaps including a large central disc, and then drill parallel holes in the sides of the can at three levels to support, starting at the bottom, a dripping tray, and two wire racks above it on which to place your food. These can rest on steel rods passed through the appropriate holes. As far as lids go, if you are using an adapted trash can, a sheet of wood will do. The smoke will escape through the holes in the side of the trash can. If you are using a trash-incinerator, it will come with a ready-made chimney in its lid. This can be blocked off with a piece of wood if you are having trouble reaching the right temperature.

Next, you stand the trash can on two large cinder blocks and place two smaller bricks just inside the cinder blocks to support a metal plate on which your sawdust will smoulder. You can easily make a metal plate by flattening a piece of corrugated iron. If this is perforated, it will make ignition easier. Finally, you place a gas burner under the metal plate to light the sawdust and maintain an appropriate temperature within the chamber during smoking. You may need to adjust the flame in the course of your smoking period. When the food is introduced into the chamber, the temperature is likely to drop, and once the sawdust gets going it will contribute heat of its own, so, other things being equal, you will want to turn down the gas a little. As with a cold smoker, a candy thermometer will allow you to monitor progress.

SOME SMOKING TIPS

Finally, some words of advice. Before you process any food in your chamber, pass smoke through it for at least 12 hours to coat it with tar deposits. This will prevent tainting. And, mindful of the fact that hot air rises, it is a good idea to swap your trays around halfway through smoking to ensure their contents receive the same amount of heat. The good news is that the hot-smoking process is immune to the outside temperature.

HOT-SMOKED CHICKEN

The first time Nick hot-smoked chicken, in his naivety he performed the operation with no brining and no initial period of cold smoking. He served the chicken hot to his guests after a three-hour smoke at 230°F and they were delighted with it. He had essentially used the hot smoker as an oven in the procedure known as smoke-roasting. The chicken was tender and juicy and only mildly smoky as the smoke didn't have much time to penetrate, plus the skin quickly dried to form a barrier.

Traditionally, hot-smoked chicken has an altogether more pronounced smoky flavor and is drier and firmer. It can be kept in the fridge for about a week or in the freezer for six months. It will revolutionize your Caesar salads.

BRINING AND DRYING
Take a medium-sized chicken and prick it down to the bone with a fork, to assist brine penetration.

Prepare an 80 percent brine (one cup salt per quart of water) and immerse the bird in it for two hours.

Dry the chicken for 24 hours in a cool, airy place. Make a loop of string, insert it under the wings, and hang the chicken from a hook.

THE SMOKING STAGES
Cold-smoke the chicken for 48 hours, making sure that the internal temperature of the cold smoker does not exceed 77°F. Then hot smoke the chicken for two hours at 230°F.

Hot-smoked chicken is well complemented by piccalilli (see page 118) and sourdough bread.

HOT-SMOKED DUCK AND GOOSE BREAST

Duck and geese may certainly be smoked whole, but we tend to limit ourselves to breasts for a variety of reasons. For one thing, you can fit more of them in the smoker. For another, there will be less molten fat to deal with. Nick found out the wisdom of this after a conflagration which consumed three sausages, a mackerel, a duck and an old pair of gardening gloves. Another advantage of using just the breasts is that the other parts of the creature can be put to better use, the legs and wings to make confit or rillettes (see page 204), and the carcasses can be roasted as the basis for excellent broths.

Both ducks and geese smoke very well. Hot-smoked "fresh" for an hour at 230°F, they make a delicious appetizer (served warm) or classy ingredient for a cassoulet (see page 192). Otherwise, they can be hot smoked in the traditional way: that is, after a period of cold-smoking. This takes longer but is definitely worth it.

The larger the breasts, the better the end results. First, prick them thoroughly and immerse them in an 80 percent brine (see page 64) for two to three hours depending on their size.

Then dry them on a rack for between 12 and 24 hours in your inactive smoker. Cold-smoke them for a good 24 hours.

Our smoking guru, Keith Erlandson, recommends exactly 36 hours at 75–80°F. Give them a little longer if it's cold outside and the temperature inside your smoker is lower than you want it.

Finish the breasts off by hot-smoking them for an hour or so at 230°F. If you vacuum seal them (see page 203), they will keep in the fridge for up to eight weeks. If you merely store them in a sealed container, you should eat them within seven days. They also freeze very well, like many smoked products, and will keep this way for up to six months.

Try either kind of breast thinly sliced in a salad with beets, new potatoes, and flat-leaf parsley.

GOOSE BREAST WITH TRUFFLE OIL

Hot-smoked goose breast is indescribably good. It has a natural affinity with another delectable item, white truffle oil (see page 132). Nick told Johnny that he had cooked this delicacy as a gourmet appetizer for a posh dinner party. "Why wasn't I invited?" demanded your ever-hungry author. "Because I only use you for experimentation purposes," Nick reminded him. **Serves 4 as a starter**

5 ounces Jerusalem artichokes, cleaned and sliced very thinly with a mandolin, or food processor (about 1–1½ cups)

Vegetable oil

A couple of handfuls of wild arugula

1 medium-sized, hot-smoked, goose breast (see left), very thinly sliced

28 fresh sage leaves, deep fried until crispy (about 1 minute)

12 walnut halves, baked in the oven for 10 minutes at 350°F

Parmesan shavings

White truffle oil (see page 132—a tiny amount goes a long way)

1 teaspoon good-quality balsamic vinegar

Cracked black pepper

- Make sure that the Jerusalem artichoke slices are so thin they are translucent, then deep-fry them in hot oil until golden and crispy. Do this in small batches. Drain on paper towels, and set aside.
- Make a mound of arugula in the middle of a large, flat, white plate, then drape slices of goose breast around it, overlapping if necessary.
- Garnish with the rest of the items. You'll only need a few drops of truffle oil, as it's pretty strong stuff, plus about a teaspoonful of balsamic vinegar.

SMOKED VENISON

Smoked venison is a great delicacy. It is among the darkest of smoked meats and has a deep, sweet flavor. It is also very low in cholesterol. However, different cuts and species of deer require different treatment. This is a complicated business, so here we restrict ourselves to the hot-smoking of fillets of boneless haunch. These can be bought from specialty food suppliers and some supermarkets. As with most hot-smoked products, venison needs brining, drying, and a period of cold smoking before it is finished off in the hot smoker.

WEIGHING, BRINING, AND DRYING
Get hold of a thick tenderloin of venison weighing 1lb., 2 oz. Immerse it in a 70 percent brine solution (one and three-quarter cups salt to two quarts water), for 45 minutes. After brining, let drip-dry for at least 12 hours, either on a rack or suspended by string.

SMOKING
Smoke the meat in in the cold smoker for at least a few days and preferably as long as a week, at 60–75°F.

Before hot smoking, the venison should be rubbed with olive or sesame oil (the latter adds a nice nutty flavor). Smoke for one to two hours at 220°F.

MATURING AND EATING
Let the venison mature for at least a day (it will freeze for up to six months), then carve it very thinly across the grain. It is good with hard-boiled eggs and beet salad.

HOT-SMOKED MACKEREL

Mackerel are treated with a certain amount of scorn in Europe, largely because they are at their best for only a few hours, which is a lot longer than it takes them to make their way to the average fishmonger. Nevertheless, their natural oiliness makes them superb candidates for the smoker. As with those to be cooked in their fresh state, you want to select firm-fleshed, beady-eyed specimens that have been out of the sea for less than 24 hours. Better still, catch and smoke your own.

Gut the mackerel thoroughly, including the gills and the main artery that runs down the spine. Immerse the fish in 70 percent brine (one and three-quarter cups salt to two quarts water) for an hour, then dry them for four hours in a cool, airy place. Hang them with loops of string either threaded through the eyes (being dead, they won't mind) or the now empty gill-plates.

Cold smoke the mackerel for eight hours at around 75°F, then finish them off with one and a half hours in the hot smoker at 203°F. You can store your mackerel in the fridge for up to a week or for up to six months in the freezer. They are wonderful with creamy horseradish (see page 69). For a nutritious brunch or breakfast, try serving them with omelettes.

SMOKED MACKEREL SOUFFLÉ

Nick enjoys sitting at vantage points staring vacantly out to sea through binoculars. On the whole this is a sad part of his life, because nothing ever seems to happen out there. But once, and only once, it did. He was perched on a crumbling cliff in Kent, England, overlooking one of the busiest shipping lanes in the world, when mackerel started to burst out of the sea. There were millions of them, turning the water white with foam as they chased a gargantuan shoal of bait fish. Nick grabbed his rod, jumped into his inflatable kayak and only returned when he couldn't stuff any more fish into the boat. Later, he made a smoked mackerel soufflé, to celebrate. **Serves 4**

1¾ cups milk
3 tablespoons butter
⅓ cup all-purpose flour
½ cup cheddar cheese, grated
6 eggs, whites separated from yolks
Pinch of grated nutmeg
Salt
¼ teaspoon ground white pepper

1 teaspoon paprika
1 tablespoon chopped flat-leaf parsley
1 tablespoon horseradish sauce (see page 69)
7 ounces smoked mackerel (see left), filleted and flaked
Large soufflé dish with a capacity of around 1½ quarts

- Preheat the oven to 350–375°F.
- Butter the soufflé dish.
- Heat the milk in a pan, while in another melt the butter, then add the flour, and stir into a paste. Gradually add the hot milk, whisking continuously to create a smooth sauce. Add the cheese and stir until it has all melted in.
- Remove the sauce from the heat, then add the egg yolks, nutmeg, salt and pepper, paprika, parsley, horseradish, and mackerel. Mix thoroughly.
- Whip the egg whites up into soft peaks. Add them to the sauce a little at a time, folding them in gently to prevent them losing their airiness.
- Spoon the sauce into the soufflé dish and bake in the oven for 20 minutes, or until risen and golden brown. Serve immediately.

SMOKED MUSSEL AND CHEDDAR PIZZA

We call this dish pizza, but there are certain ingredients you'd be unlikely to find alongside one another in Italy. Oh well, one day the Italians may begin to appreciate the wonders of modern British cuisine. Maybe they'll start with this pizza. **Serves 2–4**

THE DOUGH

3⅓ cups "00" grade
  all-purpose flour
2 teaspoons salt
1 teaspoon rapid rise yeast
2 tablespoons olive oil
1¼ cups water

THE TOPPING

⅓ cup tomato puree—see
  page 195
2 ounces semi-dried
  tomatoes—about
  ½–⅔ cup (see page 28)
1¾ cups mature cheddar,
  grated
2 tablespoons finely diced
  pancetta-style bacon
  (see page 70)
40 smoked mussels
  (see page 81)
1 teaspoon paprika
A couple of leaves of
  tarragon, removed from
  the stalk
Freshly ground black
  pepper

- First, make the dough. We always do this by hand because it is easy and fun; however it can just as easily be made in a food processor. Sift the flour into a large bowl, then mix in the salt and yeast.
- Stir in the olive oil and water with a large spoon. Turn the sticky mass out onto a floured surface and knead until it becomes smooth. Place in a bowl in a warm area and cover with a damp cloth.
- After an hour, the dough should have risen. Knead it again for one minute, then divide it into two balls. You will just need one ball for this recipe. The other one can go in the freezer.
- To make the topping, blend the tomato puree and semi-dried tomatoes, and gently boil for 15 minutes until reduced and thickened.

- To assemble the pizza, first preheat the oven to 450°F.
- Roll out the pizza dough gradually, using a little flour to prevent it sticking. See the Pissaladière recipe on page 31 for your options concerning shapes and trays.
- Spread the tomato mixture thinly onto the dough, then sprinkle the cheddar on top.
- Add a thin layer of pancetta, the mussels, and a dusting of paprika.
- Place the pizza in the hottest part of the oven and cook for 10–15 minutes until brown and bubbling.
- Garnish with tarragon and black pepper, and serve.

CRISPY SMOKED OYSTERS WITH SESAME SEEDS

If you are wary of raw oysters, and some people do find them a bit intimidating, the solution may be to smoke them. This preserves their intense, slightly metallic fishiness but transforms their texture from slippery and elusive to firm, soft, and melting. They are excellent with hot buttered toast, but also respond well to Oriental treatment. **Serves 2**

THE DIPPING SAUCE

2 teaspoons honey
2 teaspoons toasted sesame seeds (dry-fried over medium heat until lightly colored)
Juice of 1 lime
1 tablespoon sesame oil
1 tablespoon tamari
2 teaspoons finely chopped fresh ginger
2 scallions, chopped
1 sprig of cilantro, chopped

THE OYSTERS

Vegetable oil, for frying
8 lightly smoked oysters (see page 81)
2 tablespoons all-purpose flour
1 egg, lightly beaten
2 ounces medium bread crumbs (½ cup if dried, 1–1½ cups if fresh)
1 tablespoon sesame seeds

- To make the dipping sauce, combine all the ingredients and whisk together vigorously.
- Heat the oil to 356°F in a pan or deep-fat fryer.
- Coat the oysters in the flour, then dip them in the beaten egg. Mix the sesame seeds up with the bread crumbs and coat the oysters in this mixture.
- Fry the oysters in the hot oil until golden, then serve immediately with the dipping sauce.

SAUSAGES

The word "sausage" is derived from the Latin *salsus*, which means "salted." But sausages have been around for much longer than this implies. The Sumerians were making them almost five thousand years ago in Mesopotamia. A couple of millennia later, Homer mentioned them in the *Odyssey*:

PAPRIKA SALAMI

The Hungarians are the world masters of salami, flavoring it with paprika, which they are also big on. This gives the salami both sweetness and bite. Johnny once brought a magnificent example back from Budapest, but his ex-girlfriend inadvertently ruined it by popping it in the freezer. Hence the "ex."

2¼ pounds pork shoulder, roughly ground
11 ounces pork fatback, diced small
1½ teaspoons paprika
1 teaspoon ground black pepper
2 tablespoons salt
½ teaspoon cayenne pepper
1 teaspoon caraway seeds
¼ teaspoon saltpeter, or use commercial cure mix
  and consult label for quantity
¼ teaspoon acidophilus powder, or use other
  starter culture and consult label for quantity
Casings—2- to 3-inch beef middles or widest
  available hog casings

Mix the ground pork shoulder with the fatback, then add the paprika, black pepper, salt, cayenne, caraway seeds, and saltpeter or commercial cure mix. Add the starter culture, having first dissolved it in one tablespoon of water, and then mix everything together thoroughly.

Stuff the mixture into the casings. If you are using hog casings, the salamis will mature faster as they will be narrower, but they will be a little thin. You should aim to make them approximately 12 inches in length.

The next stage is to incubate the salami. This entails hanging them in a warm environment (around 86°F) for 24 hours to get the fermenting process going. Your drying box (see page 14) has all the right credentials, but you may need to leave the door or lid slightly ajar to maintain the right temperature. Place an open container of water inside to keep the environment humid.

The salamis should now be cold-smoked for two days at a temperature not exceeding 72°F. Beech wood imparts a good flavor. They will turn a deep smoky orange.

Now you can hang the salamis. Pick somewhere cool and airy, where the temperature is unlikely to rise above 54°F, and leave them for at least two months if you used hog casings or four if you used beef. Inspect them from time to time during this period—if the meat in one seems a bit loose, you can compact it and re-tie the ends. Don't be surprised if white mold appears on the surfaces of the sausages during the maturing phase. It's meant to.

Your salamis are edible when they feel firm and look dry, but you can leave them hanging for longer if you prefer them hardish. When they reach a desirable condition, you can slow down their hardening by rubbing off their surface mold with a cloth and rolling them in wood ash.

Keep your salamis cool in a pantry or fridge and eat within one month of cutting the first slices.

PICKLING

The word "pickle" has reached us, via Low Medieval German, from *peik*, an Indo-European root meaning "sharp-pointed." And sharp is exactly how pickled foods taste, due to their high acid content. This is what produces that pleasurable shudder when you first bite into a cornichon or pickled onion.

Pickling works because microbes don't like acid. Although today the term "pickling" is synonymous with long immersion in vinegar, the earliest pickles were made by fermentation (see Fermenting chapter). Bacteria occurring naturally on the surface of cucumbers, cabbages, and other suitable vegetables would, given the right conditions, convert the sugars they contained into acid. This made them last a very long time.

Alcohol exposed to the air gradually turns into acetic acid, which is the active ingredient in vinegar. In medieval Europe, malt vinegar was produced in brewing areas and wine vinegar in the vineyards of the south. The Japanese, meanwhile, made a similar product from rice liquor. People soon discovered that vinegar had an excellent preservative effect on vegetables, and also that it kept them nicely crunchy. Verjuice, the unfermented but still acidic juice of grapes or apples, was also commonly used for pickling until the nineteenth century.

In England, pickled vegetables came seriously into vogue during the sixteenth century. Increasing affluence made beer and wine products more readily available, and salted foods began to be regarded, rather snobbishly, as linked with poverty. Onions, eggs, and walnuts were the first big vinegar-pickled products, and the first two at least are still sold in many a traditional pub and fish-and-chip shop.

The most venerable pickled food, however, is the cucumber. That little slice of tangy green in your Whopper® or Big Mac™ has a very long pedigree indeed. Cucumbers originated in India, and the word "gherkin," which refers to small pickled cukes, is derived from an Aryan word, derivatives of which are shared by people as diverse as the Czechs and the Greeks. The Mesopotamians were pickling cucumbers in brine 4,500 years ago. Aristotle praised the healing effects of cucumber and Cleopatra considered them an important beauty aid. They were served at a feast thrown by King John of England in the early thirteenth century. More recently, the statesman Thomas Jefferson wrote that "on a hot day in Virginia, I know nothing more comforting than a fine spiced pickle, brought up trout-like from the sparkling depths of the aromatic jar below the stairs of Aunt Sally's cellar."

Pickles are good examples of foods that people originally grew to love through necessity rather than first impressions. Give a small child a pickled onion and you will see what we mean. The taste for this kind of food has to be acquired, but, once it's there, it is there for ever. Interestingly, the Chinese are just as convinced by the old wives' tale that pregnant women crave pickles as we are in the West.

PRESERVED LEMONS

Silky preserved lemons are an essential ingredient in Moroccan and North African cuisine. They impart a fragrant, sweet yet sour taste to tagines and salads and go particularly well with lamb and chicken. Once pickled, you can eat the whole thing, rind and all.

TO FILL A 2¼-CUP CANNING JAR
10 medium unwaxed lemons
salt
4 bay leaves
15 peppercorns
15 coriander seeds
6 cloves

Cut all the lemons in half horizontally into wedges, eight per lemon, then remove the seeds.

Squeeze the remaining lemon halves and reserve the juice.

Firmly press a layer of lemon wedges into the bottom of a sterilized jar (see page 164). Cover with two teaspoons of salt, a bay leaf, a few peppercorns and coriander seeds, and one or two cloves. Press down another layer of lemon wedges and repeat the salting and spicing process. Continue until there is only an inch or so of space at the top of the jar.

Now pour in the lemon juice, seal the jar (see page 164), and store under the stairs or in the cellar for a month before using. The lemons will keep for one year.

You may want to check the lemons every few days. Some batches let off a bit of gas and briefly opening the lids will relieve the pressure. But this problem is unlikely to occur if you've used enough salt.

SLOW-COOKED LAMB WITH PRESERVED LEMONS

This recipe demonstrates what a little bit of age does to a salted lemon. The result is an eloquent advertisement for the transformative powers of pickling: the character of the fruit is changed beyond recognition. Because the stew is so fragrant and tangy, a little goes a long way. **Serves 4–6**

1½ pounds leg of lamb
meat, cubed (about
3 cups)
5 tablespoons olive oil
2 teaspoons ground cumin
1 teaspoon ground
coriander
1½ teaspoons paprika
1½ teaspoons chopped
garlic
2 medium onions, sliced
6 medium-strength whole
dried red chiles
(see page 26)
4 cloves
½ teaspoon ground
cinnamon

2¼ cups tomato puree
(see page 195)
2 ounces semi-dried
tomatoes or a little less
sun-dried tomato, roughly
chopped—about ⅔ cup
(see page 28)
1¼ cups water
2 whole preserved lemons
or 12 wedges of
preserved lemon (see
page 104), assuming
8 wedges per fruit
A large sprig of mint,
chopped
A large sprig of parsley,
chopped
Salt

- For this recipe you need a heavy-duty, ovenproof, three-quart pan with a capacity of tight-fitting lid. It must be suitable for heating in the oven.
- Fry the cubes of lamb meat over fierce heat in one tablespoon of the olive oil until browned. This will take about five minutes. Set aside.
- Pour the remaining oil into the pan and gently simmer the cumin, coriander, paprika, and garlic for a few minutes. Then turn up the heat and toss in the onions and fry for 10–15 minutes until soft, stirring frequently.
- Add the lamb, red chiles, cloves, cinnamon, tomato puree, sun-dried tomatoes, water, and preserved lemons. Bring to a boil, then turn down to a simmer.
- Add half the mint and parsley and a little salt, then place the lid on the pan and put in a low oven (300°F) and leave it there for three to four hours, cooking gently.
- When you remove the stew from the oven, garnish it with the remaining mint and parsley. Remove the chiles and the preserved lemon wedges; they have done their work and may now be discarded.
- Serve with rice or couscous.

PICKLED ONIONS

Though not ideal if you are about to go on a date, pickled onions will awaken the most jaded of tastebuds. They will also make you ravenously thirsty, hence the traditional jar in old-time pubs. You can eat them on their own when you need pepping up, or serve them with cheese and cold cuts. Pickled pearl onions are mandatory with a cheese fondue.

The key to success is to use tiny onions and to make sure the vinegar is sweet enough. Some of our early batches were unpleasantly sharp. After much experimentation, we've found the following recipe produces the sweetest, crispest onions.

3 pounds small pickling onions
¼ cup sea salt or kosher salt
Several cloves
Several blades of mace
1–2 fresh chiles, cut in half
2 cups sugar
5 cups white wine vinegar

Trim the tops and bottoms off the onions, but don't overdo it or they will disintegrate in their pickle. Leaving the skins still on, pour boiling water over them and let them blanch for 20 seconds. Then tip out the hot water, cover with cold water, and peel them under the water. This will prevent the surfaces oxidizing and toughening up.

Layer the onions in a clean bowl, and sprinkle each layer with salt as you go. Cover with a clean cloth and leave overnight. The salt will draw out much of the onions' moisture, ensuring a desirable crunch.

Next day, rinse them well and dry them as thoroughly as possible. Place them in sterilized jars (see page 164), with two cloves, a blade of mace and half a chile in each.

Boil up the sugar and vinegar for one minute, then pour the hot liquid over the onions. Seal the jars (see pages 164) and wait two to three weeks before eating. They will keep for at least six months.

PICCALILLI

Whereas American picalilli is very sweet and contains whole mustard seeds, British picalilli is made with powdered mustard and little or no sugar, as is the case with this recipe. This version is crunchy and has a bit of a kick, which helps to explain how this bright yellow condiment got to be so popular, particularly with cheese.

We found ourselves truer to the Indian origins of this dish than we had intended when we couldn't get any pickling cucumbers on the day we planned to make it. Instead, we purchased some unfamiliar vegetables called parval and tindori, reassured by the local Indian grocer that they would do fine. He turned out to have given good advice.

TO MAKE THREE ¼-CUP CONTAINERS
- 2 pounds, 6 ounces mixed vegetables, cut into ½-inch cubes*
- 2 tablespoons salt
- 1 tablespoon turmeric powder
- ⅔ cup mustard powder
- ½ teaspoon ground white pepper
- 2 teaspoons ground ginger
- ⅓ cup all-purpose flour
- ¼ teaspoon ground nutmeg
- 5 tablespoons cider vinegar plus another ⅔ cup cider vinegar
- 1 cup malt vinegar
- a dash of water

*We use carrot, cauliflower, shallot, turnip, baby corn, parsnip, and pickling cucumber. Cauliflower is essential in anything worthy of the name "piccalilli."

Place the vegetables cubes in a large bowl and mix them with the salt. Cover and leave overnight. The salt will draw out their liquid, giving them bite and intensifying the flavors.

In a very large pot, mix the turmeric, mustard, white pepper, ginger, flour, nutmeg, and the five tablespoons of cider vinegar into a smooth paste. Slowly whisk in the rest of the vinegar, then add the vegetables, the malt vinegar and the water.

Gently heat the mixture until the sauce thickens. This should take 10–15 minutes. You must stir constantly or the flour will stick to the bottom of the pan. Remember that you don't want to actually cook the vegetables or they will lose their crunch, so take care not to over-boil.

Store your piccalilli in sterilized jars (see page 164). It will keep for six months in a cool pantry and improve with age. Once opened, refrigerate and eat within six weeks.

Serve with roast chicken or frankfurters.

HERBS, PASTES, AND INFUSED OILS AND VINEGARS

Humans have treasured herbs and spices since prehistory. Initially this was largely on account of their medicinal and preservative properties, but as time has worn on, taste alone has become the primary motive for using them. This is particularly true in parts of the world where more sophisticated drugs and preserving methods have taken over.

But the tastiness and health-enhancing properties of herbs and spices are not unrelated. The human body knows a good thing when it smells or nibbles it. And as we are starting to see, a liking for foods that were once vital to survival tends to be passed down within a culture even when their original *raison d'être* has long-since lapsed.

Herbs can, of course, be dried, but another way of using them is to combine them with oil or vinegar. Depending upon the ratio of the flavoring ingredient to its medium, this can produce a delicate infusion or a pungent paste. Often the original colors of the additives are retained, which is why pesto and mint sauce are so vividly green, and why glass-bottled infusions are so aesthetically pleasing.

Pastes, often very strong ones, are particularly important in hot areas like India, Southeast Asia, and the Mediterranean. They frequently contain antiseptic and body-cooling ingredients like chiles, and they stimulate digestion. They also coat the foods with which they are served—often noodles of one kind or another—quite deliciously. Flavored oils and vinegars make for wonderful salad dressings.

Of the two preserving mediums, vinegar is the more effective as its acidity is anathema to most bacteria. Infused vinegars, therefore, tend to keep longer than their oil equivalents. Oils can go rancid relatively quickly once exposed to the air, although the ingredients used in flavoring them often have antibacterial properties. They are also not immune to the *Botulinum* bacterium. Their lives can be extended by heating them under pressure (see Bottling and Canning chapter), but this may impair the taste. The best compromise is to keep them in the fridge and to monitor them closely for spoilage. Once they are opened, you will need to use them within a couple of weeks. Fortunately, oil-based pastes like pesto freeze very well.

Herbs are not the only foods that can be used as the basis for feisty infusions and pastes. As you will see from the recipes that follow, certain vegetables and fungi can perform similar tricks.

THAI RED AND GREEN CURRY PASTE

In the UK you can now find Thai food in out-of-the-way rustic pubs where you half expect them to still refer to Thailand as Siam. Thai cooking is taking over the world, and red and green curries are the biggest weapons in its armory.

The difference between the two kinds of paste is largely cosmetic. The red one takes its color from dried red chiles, the green from fresh green ones. As the Heinz marketing people have found with their ketchup, people are capricious—sometimes they feel like eating red, at other moments they fancy a bit of green. In Thailand the red version is usually the hotter, whereas in some European Thai restaurants the "natural" semiology is demonically reversed. If you order a green curry in France on the assumption it will be mild, you may get a similar shock to the unwary traveler there who drinks from the faucet marked "C" (in other words the hot one).

THAI CURRIES

Both our pastes are similar in strength. All you need to do with either to make an authentic Thai meal is combine it with fresh chicken stock, coconut milk, and shredded chicken or seafood. But unlike the ready-made pastes available in Oriental grocers, ours are heat-treated to give them long lives. They will keep in the fridge for at least six months.

RED CURRY PASTE (MAKES 1 POUND, 2 OUNCES)

Zest of 2 limes
1 medium head of garlic, cloves peeled
3 ounces whole lemongrass, roughly chopped
15 dried medium-strength red chiles, stalks removed and soaked in warm water for 20 minutes
6 fresh bird's eye chiles
4 ounces galangal, peeled and roughly chopped (about ½ cup)
3 ounces cilantro roots with a little stalk (about ⅓ bunch), washed thoroughly
4 ounces shallots (about 1 cup), peeled and roughly chopped
1 tablespoon shrimp powder or 1 teaspoon belachan (fermented shrimp paste)
1 level tablespoon ground cumin
1 teaspoon freshly ground black pepper
2 tablespoons sesame oil
¼ cup vegetable oil

Place the lime zest, garlic, lemongrass, reconstituted dry chiles, fresh chiles, galangal, cilantro roots, shallots, and shrimp powder or belachan in a food processor and blend until smoothish.

PESTO

The medieval Genoans are said to have created pesto in imitation of the crushed walnut sauces they sampled while operating trading posts in the Black Sea. Back in the Mediterranean, they replaced the walnuts with pine nuts and found they had the perfect lubricant for their pasta.

The essence of pesto is its simplicity. Why then is the store-bought kind so often disappointing? Nick knows the answer, having been to the factories where they make it. Commercially produced pestos are based on dried or frozen basil, hence their lack of character. You are much better off making your own. In the UK, September is the time to do it, when your home-grown basil is bushy and bursting with fragrant oils.

4 ounces fresh basil leaves
Juice of 2 medium lemons
1 cup Italian pine nuts, dry-roasted in a frying pan
   until lightly colored
¼ teaspoon salt
4 cloves of garlic, peeled
⅔ cup olive oil
2 cups finely grated Parmesan
Freshly ground black pepper

Blend the basil, lemon juice, pine nuts, salt, garlic, and olive oil until the mixture resembles the texture of couscous. Transfer to a bowl using a spatula, then stir in the Parmesan and black pepper. Easy or what?

The pesto can be stored in a sterilized airtight container (see page 164) in the fridge for up to two weeks, or you can freeze it for up to six months.

If you are feeling adventurous, you could try replacing the basil with another herb such as cilantro or parsley. The pine nuts are also negotiable; toasted almonds or walnuts could be substituted.

Pesto is particularly good with penne as it sticks to their convoluted surfaces. Try it sprinkled with a few crispy cubes of pancetta (see page 70).

WARM CHICKEN PASTA SALAD WITH PESTO

This versatile salad can be eaten warm or cold, as an appetizer or in a picnic. It is very easy to make, hence the shortness of the list of ingredients. The pesto here is slightly different from the one we showed you how to make on the opposite page in that it contains roasted rather than raw garlic. This gives it a mellower, sweeter taste. Making pesto is a perfect way to use up your summer herbs before the frost kills them. **Serves 4**

THE PESTO
As per recipe on page 126, but replace the raw garlic cloves with half the pulp from a roasted head of garlic
Dribble of olive oil

THE SALAD
2 large chicken breasts, cut into long strips, seasoned with salt, pepper, and lemon juice
1 tablespoon olive oil
3 ounces wild arugula (about a couple of large handfuls), washed
7 ounces dried penne pasta (about 2½–2¾ cups), cooked, then coated in a little olive oil
A few toasted pine nuts
Cracked black pepper

- To roast the garlic, tear off a sheet of aluminum foil, and place an entire head on it with the top sliced off. Pour a dribble of olive oil into the garlic and wrap the foil around it. Roast at 425°F for 30 minutes or until soft. Let cool, then squeeze out the sweet pulp. Add half of it to the other pesto ingredients and blend. You'll be left with more than you need for this recipe, so store the excess in the fridge.
- Fry the chicken breasts in one tablespoon of olive oil over medium heat until nicely browned, turning them over as you go. This should take about five minutes.
- Mix together all the salad ingredients in a large bowl along with two heaped tablespoons of pesto.
- Season with a little cracked black pepper.

SUN-DRIED TOMATO PASTE

Sun-dried tomato paste is tastier than regular tomato paste and every bit as versatile. It can be used in much the same way, for instance, as a pizza topping or an ingredient in Bolognese sauce, but also has applications all its own. Try it in a sandwich with Gruyère cheese and sweet-cured ham.

To make the paste, you can either use genuine sun-dried tomatoes or "fully dried" ones as per our instructions on page 28.

4 ounces sun-dried tomatoes (about 1–1½ cups)
1 medium head of garlic, roasted
⅔ cup olive oil
½ teaspoon salt
½ teaspoon dried oregano

Place the sun-dried tomatoes in a small pan and just cover them with water. Simmer for 10 minutes, then let them soak for 20 minutes more. Pat them dry with paper towels.

Roast the garlic according to the instructions on page 127.

Blend all the ingredients together until smooth. Store the paste in the fridge in a sterilized airtight container (see page 164) for up to three months.

"SUPER" HARISSA PASTE

Like all the pastes in this chapter, harissa captures the distinctive flavors of its homeland in a highly convenient form. In this case, the region of origin is North Africa. The harissa sold in the local souks is a fiery, pared-down version which needs rounding out at home with additional herbs and seasonings. Nick has simplified matters by adding the extras at the paste stage.

For a gourmet meal, simply fry up some lamb with onions and a dollop of this paste, add tomatoes and some stock, and serve with fluffy couscous.

2 ounces medium-strength dried cayenne chiles
(about 1¼–1¾ cups)*
½ cup olive oil
5 cloves of garlic, peeled
1 tablespoon ground cumin
1 tablespoon ground coriander
1 teaspoon caraway seeds
Juice of 1 lemon
1 ounce fresh mint leaves (about 1¼–1¾ cups)
1 ounce fresh parsley leaves (about 1¼–1¾ cups)
1 ounce fresh cilantro leaves (about 1¼–1¾ cups)
2 teaspoons salt

* You could also use guajillo chiles, which have a fiery licorice flavor.

Remove the stalks from the dried chiles, then soak them in hot water for 30 minutes. Blend them with the remaining ingredients until you have a smooth paste.

Store in the fridge in a sterilized airtight container (see page 164) for up to one month, or in the freezer for up to six months.

TAPENADE

Tapenade is a pungent, salty specialty of the French Riviera (*tapeno* is the Provençal word for caper). There is something ancient about the flavor, yet amazingly, tapenade was invented in the late nineteenth century by a chef at the Maison Dorée in Marseilles.

This recipe is more substantial than some versions as it incorporates chopped tuna. Try it with seared fish steaks, a roasted vegetable salad, or stuffed into tomatoes. Alternatively, serve the tapenade as a dip with pita bread.

2 cups black olives, pits removed
10 anchovy fillets, rinsed first if preserved in salt
  (see page 45)
⅓ cup capers, rinsed before use if preserved
  in salt (see page 52)
2 cloves of garlic, chopped
1 ounce fresh basil (about 1¼–1¾ cups)
Leaves from about 3 sprigs of fresh thyme
3 ounces tuna canned in brine, drained (about ½ cup)
1 teaspoon Dijon mustard
⅔ cup olive oil
2 tablespoons lemon juice
Ground black pepper

Place the olives, anchovies, capers, garlic, basil, and thyme leaves in a food processor and blend until grainy in texture.

Chop the tuna quite finely and add it to the blended mixture with the mustard, olive oil, lemon juice, and black pepper.

Mix thoroughly with a wooden spoon and put in a sterilized jar (see page 164). It will keep for up to one month in the fridge.

SUN-DRIED TOMATO SOUP WITH TAPENADE

It isn't easy to make a really good tomato soup, but we think we may have achieved it here. We were thinking of selling the recipe to Heinz, but we've decided to give it to you instead. **Serves 4**

4 ounces carrots, sliced
  (about ¾–1 cup)
4 ounces celery, sliced
  (about 1 cup)
6 ounces onions, sliced
  (about 1–1¼ cups)
2 tablespoons butter
4 teaspoons olive oil
4 cups vegetable broth
½ cup all-purpose flour
¾ cup tomato paste

1½ ounces sun-dried
  tomatoes (see page 28),
  simmered in water for 10
  minutes until soft
A pinch of white pepper
1 teaspoon salt
A pinch of allspice
A pinch of ground bay leaf
2 teaspoons cider vinegar
3 tablespoons sugar
25 fresh basil leaves
⅔ cup fresh heavy cream
4 ounces tapenade—about
  ½ cup (see left)

- In a good-sized pan, fry the carrot, celery, and onion in the butter and olive oil over medium heat until soft.
- Heat the vegetable broth in a separate pan.
- Add the flour and the tomato paste to the fried vegetables and stir in well. Then turn the heat down and start adding the hot vegetable broth. Do this gradually, stirring constantly to make a smooth soup.
- When all the broth is incorporated, add the sun-dried tomatoes, pepper, salt, allspice, ground bay leaf, vinegar, and sugar, and simmer for 15 minutes.
- Add the basil, and using an immersion blender, blend until smooth. Then stir in the cream.
- Serve in soup plates. Garnish with tapenade and have hunks of baguette ready on the side.

ADOBO

If you've followed our advice on page 27 and smoke-dried some jalapeño chiles to turn them into chipotles, this is what to do with them next. Although the Filipinos confusingly use the term "adobo" for a stew made with soy sauce and garlic, for us it will always remain this delectable Mexican vinegar paste.

Adobo works equally well as a marinade or a sauce base, and it gives a definite lift to items destined for the barbecue. Use it as a marinade for beef and pork.

You don't have to stick to chipotles when making adobo, even within a single batch. Winning alternatives include the pasilla or "raisin chile," shiny, curved, and mildly spicy, and the gently hot ancho, the mature, red, heart-shaped form of the poblano chile. If you haven't got around to growing your own, Mexican chiles are readily available through mail-order companies and specialty shops.

**MAKES ABOUT 12 OUNCES OF PASTE,
ENOUGH FOR 2 MEXICAN FEASTS**

- 1 medium head of garlic
- 1 teaspoon olive oil
- 2 chipotle chiles (see page 27), slit open and seeds removed
- 5 ancho chiles, slit open and seeds removed
- 1 teaspoon cumin seeds and 1 teaspoon coriander seeds, dry-fried in a pan until lightly colored
- 1 ounce fresh oregano leaves (about 1¼ cups)
- 2 shallots, peeled and roughly chopped
- 1 teaspoon ground cinnamon
- 2 teaspoons salt
- ½ cup red wine vinegar
- ½ cup balsamic vinegar

To roast the garlic, slice the top off the head to expose the flesh and dribble the olive oil into it. Wrap the garlic in foil and bake in a 425°F oven for 25–30 minutes or until soft. Let cool, then squeeze the pulpy flesh out into a bowl.

Blend the chipotle and ancho chiles with the dry-fried cumin and coriander seeds until smooth. Add the oregano, roasted garlic, and shallots, and continue to blend until they have been incorporated.

Mix in the rest of the ingredients and stir it into a paste.

Store in the fridge for up to six months in a sterilized airtight container (see page 164).

BARBECUED CHICKEN IN ADOBO

Adobo is made for summer. Its spicy oiliness makes it an excellent marinade for chicken, particularly when it's heading for the barbecue or being broiled. Serve this up with a black bean salsa and you have a satisfying and authentic Mexican meal. **Serves 4**

4 chicken legs
3 ounces adobo paste—
  about ⅓ cup (see left)

THE SALSA
5 ounces dried black beans
  (about ¾ cup), soaked
  overnight in water
1 red jalapeño chile, seeds
  removed and finely
  chopped
1 green jalapeño chile,
  seeds removed and finely
  chopped

1 large red onion, chopped
Juice and zest of 1 lime
1 tablespoon olive oil
1 small bunch of fresh
  oregano, chopped
1 small bunch of cilantro,
  chopped
1 teaspoon honey
A splash of red wine
  vinegar

- Marinate the chicken legs in the adobo paste for at least four hours prior to cooking.
- Drain, then boil the soaked black beans in enough water to comfortably cover them and simmer until soft. This will take about 45 minutes. Drain the beans and refresh with cold water.
- Place the drained beans in a large bowl along with the chiles, onion, lime juice and zest, olive oil, oregano, cilantro, honey, and vinegar. Stir thoroughly and store in the fridge until the chicken is ready.
- Cook the chicken over a barbecue until somewhat charred on each side. It must be cooked right through, underdone chicken being a no-no from the perspective of both hygiene and taste.
- Spoon a large portion of salsa onto each plate and serve with the chicken. If you also provide soft flour tortillas, your guests will be able to roll their own enchiladas.

TRUFFLE BUTTER

If you ever find yourself in possession of a fresh white "Alba" truffle, we'd frankly advise you to use it immediately. Its perfume, initially almost indescribably intense, will fade by the hour. This is one of the reasons truffles are so expensive, but a little goes a long way, and if you find yourself with any left over, you could do a lot worse than transform it into this butter. Nick learned this the hard way. He made it his life's work to harness the powerful but transient flavor of *Tuber magnatum pico*. Every November he'd spend all his Christmas money on a few small nuggets of white truffle. He'd carry them around in his pocket, burbling to strangers about how he was going to turn them into gold, and overstimulating every goat and pig within miles. Then he'd go home and turn his kitchen into a laboratory.

He tried heating truffles to exactly 154°F. He soaked them in alcohol and froze them in oil and everything in between. All in vain. In the end, his truffle dealer put him out of his misery— this is our friend, Mike de Stroumillo. Nick's obsession had been a nice little sideline for Mike, but news of yet another hundred pound's worth (in money, not weight) going up the chimney was too much for his conscience. "Look, have you tried preserving them in butter?" he asked with a sigh. So Nick did. He served the truffle butter with artichoke hearts and homemade pancetta, and his hairy brother-in-law came over all amorous.

WHITE TRUFFLE BUTTER IS THIS SIMPLE TO MAKE
  ½ ounce (10g) fresh white truffle, finely chopped
  1 cup plus 2 tablespoons (2¼ sticks) unsalted butter, at room temperature

Thoroughly mix the truffle into the butter. Portion into an ice tray, then store in the fridge for up to a week or in the freezer for up to three months.

TRUFFLE OIL
You can also flavor oil with white truffle (see photo opposite). To do this, immerse ultra-thin slices of the fungus in a neutrally flavored oil such as rapeseed oil (canola oil). Do this at the proportion of five slices per half-cup oil. Unfortunately, the taste will deteriorate after a few days whatever you do. Such is the way of the elusive truffle...

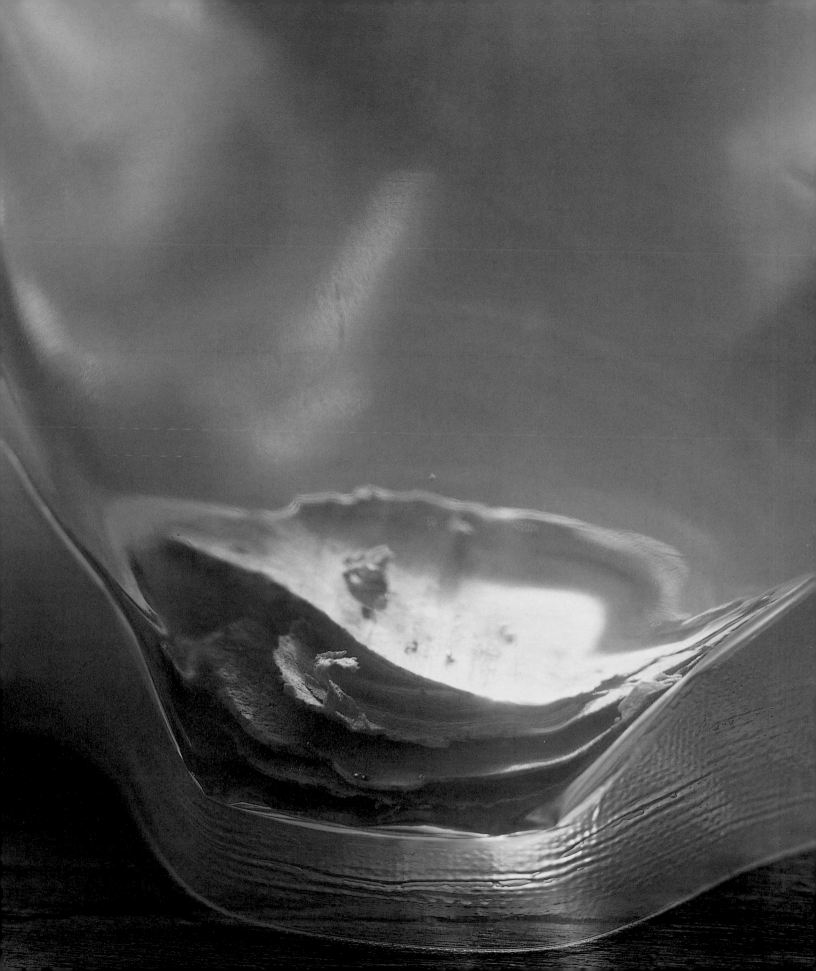

CHILI OIL

Chili oil is a luxurious way of adding fire to a dish. You can drizzle it on a pizza, incorporate it into a salad dressing, or use it as a cooking medium for a punchy stir-fry. One of the beauties of chili oil is that its flavor stands up well to high temperatures.

There are a number of ways to make it. The simplest is just to immerse whole chiles in oil, puncturing them with a pin if you want them to sink. A slightly more sophisticated way of making chili oil is the following:

18 ounces mild red chiles, seeded
1 cup olive oil or other neutral oil, e.g., corn

Run the chiles through a juice extractor, then reduce the juice in a saucepan until it darkens and starts to thicken. You are aiming to reduce its volume by approximately 90 percent.

Add the thickened chile juice to the oil and funnel it into a sterilized bottle (see page 164). It will keep in the fridge for up to one month.

HORSERADISH OIL

Horses are lucky in our opinion. Their radishes are are lot more interesting than "human" ones. This oil packs quite a kick and is surprisingly versatile. Naturally it is excellent drizzled on roast beef, but Nick enjoys it with cheese on toast. You could even use it as an alternative to wasabi mustard, mixing it with soy sauce to make a dip for sushi or sashimi.

1 cup oil*
1 small horseradish root, peeled, then thinly sliced or cut into julienne strips

*The best oils to use are neutral in taste, such as corn or sunflower oil. You could, however, mix in a dash of toasted sesame oil to give the finished product an appealing nuttiness.

Mix the oil with the horseradish, then store in a sterilized airtight container (see page 164) in the fridge for up to two months.

LEMON OIL

The most obvious way to use this oil is as the basis for a lemony salad dressing, but as usual your imagination is the only limit. The flavor combines very well with fish and lamb.

Zest of 4 lemons
2¼ cups olive oil or neutral oil such as sunflower oil

Combine the lemon zest with the oil, then store in a sterilized airtight container (see page 164) in the fridge for up to six months.

ROASTED GARLIC OIL

This is a great way of preserving roast garlic for dressings, sauces, and marinades. The ratio of garlic to oil is quite high, so this is more of a paste than an infusion. It is nice and sweet and very convenient.

2 medium heads of garlic, roasted
1 cup olive oil, plus 2 teaspoons for drizzling

To roast the garlic, slice the tops off the heads to expose the flesh and dribble a teaspoon of olive oil onto each. Wrap them in foil and bake in a 425°F oven for 25–30 minutes or until soft. Let cool, then squeeze out the pulpy flesh into a bowl.

Combine the garlic with the remaining olive oil and store in the fridge in a sterilized airtight container (see page 164) for up to three months.

This paste is excellent for basting roast meat, for instance, chicken. Just add lemon juice and a little tarragon. On table-tennis nights, we're particularly fond of slow-roast pork belly with rosemary, sage, and roasted garlic oil.

FENNEL OIL

There's something thought-provoking about the affinity between fish and fennel. The two species have precisely nothing to do with each other while they are alive, yet they taste as though they were made for each other.

Using fennel to flavor oil is a good way of capturing its licoricey essence. Serve it with poached cod or salmon.

2 heaped tablespoons fennel seeds
1¾ cups light olive oil

Grind the fennel seeds in a spice mill or spice grinder attachment of a food processor, then combine with one tablespoon of warm water and stir until it forms a paste.

Mix the paste into the oil, then leave for a few days, stirring occasionally.

Carefully pour the oil through cheesecloth into a sterilized airtight container (see page 164), leaving the sediment behind.

Store in the fridge for up to six months.

COD IN FENNEL OIL

"You must be mad!" shouted Johnny. "You can't deep-fry cod without batter, especially not in fennel oil!" "I am NOT deep-frying the cod! I'm slowly poaching it," Nick explained with a sigh. "This oil is the perfect cooking medium for chunky cod fillets like this one. Using it allows the aniseed aroma of the fennel to permeate deep into the flaky flesh." Then he fed Johnny a forkful to shut him up. Serves 2

2 chunky cod fillets
Some kitchen string
Fennel oil (see left)—
** enough to cover the fish**
** in the pan, probably**
** around 1½ cups**

Salt
Cracked black pepper
A splash of lemon juice

- Tie up the cod fillets as if you were wrapping parcels, bunching the meat up until they are vaguely box-shaped. The string should be firm but not tight. Its function is to hold the fish together during the poaching process.
- Pour the fennel oil into a non-stick frying pan, then lower in the fish fillets.
- Gently heat the oil to somewhere between (175–195°F). A food thermometer will prove more than handy here. Simmer the fish at this temperature for 15 minutes until cooked through.
- Before you gently lift the fillets out of the pan, make sure that the accompaniments are ready. We recommend serving the cod with mashed potato and fine green beans.
- Lay the fish on the potato and season with salt, pepper, and a squeeze of lemon juice. It is great with aioli, a garlicky mayonnaise made with olive oil.

RASPBERRY VINEGAR

Raspberry vinegar (see photo on page 120) is often used for making pleasantly sweet salad dressings. Try it heated with butter and poured onto broiled or fried fish. Alternatively, use it with a dash of port to de-glaze a roasting pan before making gravy in it.

2 pounds fresh or frozen raspberries (about 6 cups)
2½ cups red wine vinegar

Place half the raspberries in a bowl and cover with the vinegar. Cover with a cloth and leave for five to seven days in a warm place, stirring occasionally. Then strain the liquid, pour it over the rest of the raspberries, and cover and leave as before. Strain into sterilized bottles (see page 164), adding a few whole berries for visual effect. Wait at least one month before using.

TARRAGON VINEGAR

Tarragon goes remarkably well with fish and chicken, so tarragon vinegar is ideal as a basis for dressings to accompany said beasts. It also looks good and can be used to make classy tartare, bearnaise, and hollandaise sauces.

1 ounce fresh tarragon leaves (about 1¼–1¾ cups)
2½ cups white wine vinegar

Bruise the tarragon to release its essential oils, pack it into a jar and pour in the vinegar. Seal and shake thoroughly. Leave in a warm place for two to three weeks before using, shaking every day.

Strain through cheesecloth into a sterilized bottle and seal, (see page 164). Store in a dark cupboard for up to one year.

SALMON WITH TARRAGON VINEGAR HOLLANDAISE

In the absence of salmon, this hollandaise would be equally delicious with sea or rainbow trout. This version is unusually stable for such a notoriously fickle sauce: you can store it in the fridge for up to a week. It's also much easier to make than cooking lore would suggest. **Serves 4**

THE HOLLANDAISE
1½ cups milk
1 cup cream
¼ cup cornstarch
A pinch of cayenne pepper
A pinch of white pepper
½ teaspoon salt
¼ cup lemon juice
½ cup egg yolks
  (roughly 5 yolks)
1 tablespoon tarragon
  vinegar
⅓ cup (¾ stick) butter

THE SALMON
4 salmon fillets, skinned or scaled, and scored, seasoned with a little salt, black pepper, and a dusting of flour
1 tablespoon butter, clarified if you're feeling pernickety, plus an extra pat of butter
Juice of ½ a lemon
Some sprigs of chopped tarragon leaves

- Pour the milk and cream into a saucepan along with the cornstarch, cayenne pepper, white pepper, salt, and lemon juice. Whisk the mixture constantly as you slowly heat it. Once the cornstarch has thickened, cook for another minute, then remove the pan from heat.
- Immediately whisk in the egg yolks and the vinegar, then briefly return the pan to the heat (for less than a minute).
- Stir in the butter, and the hollandaise is ready to serve. Store any excess in an airtight container in the fridge; it will keep for up to one week.
- Using a non-stick pan, fry the salmon in one tablespoon of butter over medium heat for around four minutes on each side. Remove the fillets from the pan and place them on plates.
- Heat up the extra pat of butter in the same pan until it has boiled off but hasn't started to burn, then squeeze in the lemon juice. The butter will fizz up. Pour it over the salmon.
- Serve with the hollandaise sauce and garnish with the chopped tarragon leaves.

FERMENTING

Most of the techniques in this book are aimed at the suppression of micro-organisms. Fermenting is different. In the fifth century B.C.E., the Greek author Herodotus captured the essential strangeness of this approach when he wrote in amazement, "All men are afraid of their food spoiling, but the Egyptians make dough which has to be spoiled."

He was referring to the miracle of leavening. The locals had learned that yeast, which formed spontaneously on crushed dates and figs, somehow dramatically inflated their breads.

As with other preserving methods, most of the benefits of fermentation were probably discovered by accident. The Koreans have a legend in which a poor farmer puts some withered old cabbages in a bowl of sea water to revive them. When he looks at them a couple of hours later, he is overjoyed to discover they have swollen magnificently. This is matched by his disappointment the next day when he returns to find them limp and even smaller than they were to begin with. But there is a consolation: they taste delicious. A similar revelation occurred when a forgotten tub of fruit turned out to have decomposed into a juice which was good to drink and caused a pleasant intoxication. Or when a bird left hanging for a few days proved tastier and more tender than ones eaten immediately.

The fermented specialities of some parts of the world may smack of desperation to cosseted urban Westerners, but the people who depended on them grew to adore them. A case in point is Norwegian *rakfisk*, traditionally made by burying tubs of oily fish in the soil, where they ferment in their own enzymes. The end result is overpowering to the unaccustomed. The same can be said of Sudanese *um tibay*. This is made by finely chopping an entire gazelle (hooves, bones, offal, nerves, the lot), stuffing the mixture into the animal's stomach and leaving it to hang on a tree for a few days where it ferments in the super-hot sun. Then it is cooked in hot ashes, cut into strips, and dried. Nothing is allowed to go to waste.

Fermentation has an astonishing range of practical applications, from compost-making to the manufacture of synthetic rubber. In the field of food and drink, it is used for making so many kinds of product that a line must be drawn somewhere or we could go on forever. Accordingly, in this chapter we are going to ignore brewing, baking, and the fermentation of dairy products. But just imagine how different the course of history would have been had people never developed these ways of exploiting microbial activity.

In the meantime, there are plenty of excellent fermented products you can make at home. We've already shown you how to make two meat ones: paprika salami and garlic sausage (see pages 90 and 93). Here we teach you to prepare four more classic fermented foods. Cumulatively they illustrate what fermenting is all about: harnessing natural processes to produce diverse and amazing transformations. If you find yourself addicted to this rewarding form of alchemy, there are endless avenues to explore.

THE PRINCIPLES OF FERMENTING

The basic idea in fermenting is to promote the growth of certain bacteria, molds, or yeasts which produce something useful as a by-product of their life-sustaining activities. This varies from carbon dioxide (the key to making bread rise) to alcohol (obviously handy when it comes to brewing) to lactic acid (the secret behind cheese-making and the long lives of cured sausages). Many of these substances in turn inhibit the growth of unwanted beasties. They also give fermented foods their characteristic flavors. To get the balance right, however, you need to be precise in your preparations.

The first requirement, as ever, is hygiene. All tools and vessels used in fermenting must be properly sterilized to prevent the end-products from spoiling. The next imperative is to give the benign organisms something to eat. One way or another, this is usually sugar. Fortunately, this tends to be present in the food you are trying to preserve, for example, as glucose and fructose in vegetables, and lactose in milk products.

The final part of the jigsaw is storage. Conditions must be right for the "good" organisms to proliferate, thereby swamping potential undesirables. The food must be properly sealed, and the pH (acidity) of its environment may need to be adjusted, often with vinegar. Salt may be added to inhibit the growth of "bad" bacteria. Then it is primarily a matter of keeping the food at the right temperature. Too cold and the benign organisms will reproduce too slowly. Too hot and they may go bananas. If this happens, the end-products will be unpalatable at best and at worst downright dangerous. Fortunately, the tell-tale signs are hard to miss. These include alarming discoloration, abundant mold growth, and repugnant aromas (although sauerkraut and kimchee don't smell great at the best of times).

For the majority of fermenting processes, a temperature of between 59–68°F is ideal. We'll give you full instructions for the preparation of the items covered in this chapter as we come to them.

SAUERKRAUT

Although it is now most closely linked with Germany, fermented sliced cabbage has been a part of life in the Far East for thousands of years. The strange truth is that the men who built the Great Wall of China subsisted largely on sauerkraut. The chief difference is that theirs was fermented in rice wine, whereas the German kind relies on salt. Fermented cabbage appears to have been brought to the West by migrating Central Asian tribes and the armies of Genghis Khan.

Sauerkraut proved immensely popular in central and northern Europe, and later in the colder parts of North America. Cabbages were easy to grow, preserving them was straightforward, and the end-product was rich in vitamin C. Sauerkraut was particularly valuable in the winter when fresh fruits and vegetables were unavailable. The British Navy equipped its ships with barrels of it to ward off scurvy.

As with many popular fermented foods, the chemical work underlying sauerkraut is done by lactobacillus bacteria. These microbes convert the natural sugars in the cabbage to lactic acid, helping to preserve it and giving the finished product its characteristic sour tang.

There is no point pretending sauerkraut smells great as it's cooking, but the finished item is lip-smackingly tasty. Try it with homemade frankfurters (page 97).

TO MAKE SAUERKRAUT

Two heads of cabbage will yield quite enough sauerkraut for your immediate needs:

> 1 very large container, preferably glass or enamel,
>   but plastic will do
> 2 heads of cabbage
> Sea salt or kosher salt

Clean and sterilize the container by pouring boiling water down the sides and letting it sit for a few minutes.

Remove the core from the cabbages, then cut them into quarters and finely shred them. Food processors do this well.

Weigh the cabbage and add one heaped tablespoon of salt per pound. Mix them together thoroughly in the fermenting container. The salt will soon start to draw the juices from the cabbage, which will ferment in its own brine.

To make sure the cabbage stays immersed in it, weigh them down with plastic food bags filled with brine made with one tablespoon of salt per quart of water. If the bags leak a little, the cabbage won't be watered down. Alternatively, use a plate weighed down with a jar of water, as in the photo opposite.

Cover the container with plastic wrap or wrap it in a heavy cloth. Then leave it in a dark place to ferment for six weeks at ambient temperature (64°F).

When the the sauerkraut is ready, decant it into sterilized jars, seal (see page 164) and store them in the fridge for up to six months. Alternatively, you can bottle it (see chapter 10) in which case it will keep for one year. To do this, drain off the juice, heat it to boiling point, then re-add the cabbage and simmer for five minutes. Transfer the sauerkraut and juice into sterilized canning jars and process in boiling water (see page 190), for 25 minutes. Cool at room temperature and store under the stairs or in a cellar.

BRAISED PORK WITH SAUERKRAUT

This rich Bavarian favorite is best made with a thick cut of pork belly. As you eat it, you can almost hear the slapping of palms on lederhosen-clad thighs. Sauerkraut and apple is a classic sweet-and-sour combination, and as both the Chinese and Germans have discovered, sweet-and-sour goes very well with pork. This is a warming dish for a cold winter's evening. **Serves 4**

10 fresh sage leaves
2 tart cooking apples or
  Granny Smiths, peeled
  and chopped
4 cloves
4 cloves of garlic, chopped
1 tablespoon Dijon mustard
2 tablespoons brown sugar
11 ounces sauerkraut—
  about 1¼ –1½ cups
  (see page 144), drained
1 cup chicken broth
½ cup beer
A thick cut of pork belly,
  about 3¼ pounds
Salt
Pepper

- Preheat the oven to 350°F.
- Place the sage leaves, apples, cloves, garlic, mustard, brown sugar, sauerkraut, chicken broth, and beer in an ovenproof dish and mix thoroughly.
- Add the pork belly, skin side up. Press the meat in firmly so that it nestles among the other ingredients. Then season with salt and pepper.
- Bake in the oven for three hours until the pork is soft and tender.

- Remove the pork belly and place it in a clean ovenproof dish. Finish it off under a hot broiler for ten minutes to crisp up the skin. Alternatively, turn the oven up to 425–450°F and roast the belly for a further 15 minutes.
- Shred the pork into the sauerkraut mix and serve with baked potatoes.

KIMCHEE

Kimchee is a generic term for any spicy, Korean, fermented, pickled vegetables. Johnny's wife, Percy, is no one's idea of a Korean, but she did manage to get seriously addicted to kimchee. It suited her fiery nature. On one occasion, she bought a tub in Chinatown in London, took it back to her office, and popped it in a drawer. Then she went off to a meeting. When she got back, the kimchee was gone. It had been escorted from the building by Security. A nervous colleague had complained about the smell.

Kimchee, particularly the cabbage variety, can indeed whiff a bit. In this, it is only obeying the law common among fermented foods of smelling one way while tasting quite another. This is what makes kimchee an acquired taste. The initial reaction is usually negative, but it is later overruled when the benefits come to light (though not by everyone). The same is true of whiskey, blue cheese, and gentleman's relish. Persevere with kimchee and you may find you can't live without it.

They eat literally hundreds of kinds of kimchee in Korea. The most popular revolve around cucumber, turnips, and cabbage, and are made with mind-blowing quantities of salt and hot red pepper powder. Fermented shrimp or oysters are often added to the mix. This recipe is a somewhat toned-down introduction to the genre.

TO MAKE 1 LARGE JAR

    2¼ pounds bok choy or Chinese cabbage
    Pickling salt or table salt
    3 cloves of garlic, peeled and chopped
    2 teaspoons chopped fresh ginger
    3 medium-strength hot red chiles, finely chopped
    1 small bunch of scallions, chopped
    2 teaspoons sugar
    2 tablespoons fish sauce
    1 tablespoon soy sauce

Separate the leaves of the bok choy or Chinese cabbage and wash them well. Then either tear or roughly chop them into small pieces and scoop into a large bowl.

Dissolve three tablespoons of salt into three cups of water and pour it over the greens. Make sure all the greens are immersed in the brine by weighing them down with something, for instance, a plate with a large bottle of water on top.

Leave the bok choy/cabbage in the brine for eight hours, then drain it off and immerse them in fresh cold water for 10 minutes. Then drain off this water, too.

Now that the greens have been cured and rehydrated, they are ready to ferment. Place them in a tall, sterilized glass jar (see page 164) and make up the liquor. Take two and three-quarters cups water and mix in one and a half tablespoons of salt plus the garlic, ginger, chiles, scallions, sugar, and the fish and soy sauces. Make sure the salt is completely dissolved, then pour the mixture over the greens in the jar, taking care to cover them completely. Seal in line with the instructions on page 164.

Leave the jar in a warm room (above 75°F) for 24 hours. Then refrigerate the kimchee for up to one month.

Nick once made a deranged fusion dish with this kimchee. He fried some boiled diced potato in oil with onion, garlic, and diced pancetta, then added potted shrimp, bok choy, kimchee, and petite peas. The result was unique and startlingly delicious.

MISO

Someone coming across miso for the first time will probably have no idea what it is made from. All they will see is a yellow or brown paste. When they taste it, they will find it unlike anything they have eaten before, grainy, salty, and bursting with *umami*. The Japanese have long known about this "fifth" fundamental taste (the others are sweet, salty, sour, and bitter), but only recently has science proven the existence of a tastebud receptor for it. Umami-rich foods are savory and keep you coming back or more, and this is certainly true of miso.

The answer to the riddle is that miso is made from soybeans. These are boiled, then mixed with cooked rice or barley inoculated with the spore of a fungus called *Aspergillus oryzae*. Salt is added, then the mixture is packed into wooden vats and left to mature for between six months and two years. Every year, some 600,000 tonnes of miso are produced in Japan. That's almost 11 pounds for every man, woman, and child.

THE STARTER CULTURE

One component you are unlikely to have in your fridge is the aspergillus, the key to making the *koji* (starter culture). Fortunately, the same mold is used in making sake, and it is readily available from home-brewing stores and websites, Chinese pharmacies, and some Oriental grocery stores. You can buy it from G.E.M Cultures in California (www.gemcultures.com).

MAKING MISO

Miso comes in a range of colors and sweetnesses that reflect different soy/grain combinations. This recipe below produces a versatile light brown paste that is excellent in soups and dressings. You will end up with a lot of miso, but it will keep in the fridge for a year. The beans can be bought in Oriental and health food stores.

> 3 pounds, 6 ounces short-grain rice (about 7½–8 cups)
> Koji starter culture (*Aspergillus oryzae*), according to package instructions
> 3 pounds, 6 ounces fresh soy beans
> 1 pound, 7 ounces sea salt or kosher salt
> A sterilized cloth—this can be done by boiling it

Wash the rice in water and let it soak overnight. Place it in a strainer or colander to drip-dry for four hours, then steam it until cooked (this will take around 20 minutes). Cool it by tossing it in the air. For a good *koji*, the rice particles must be soft and elastic, dry on the surface but wet inside.

When the rice has cooled down to 77–86°F, add a small amount of the fungi spore, mixing well to distribute it. Then spread out the cloth and make small piles of rice on it, each about four inches high. After about 10 hours, the piles will start to heat up, a sure sign that the fungus is growing. You need to control their temperature for about 40 hours, keeping it between 95–104°F and taking care that it doesn't rise beyond this upper limit. To do this, you adjust the size of the rice piles. If you make them them less deep, the temperature will fall and vice versa. When the incubation period is over, you may be able to see feathery white fibers of fungus on individual grains of rice.

PREPARING THE SOYBEANS

Soak the soybeans overnight, then boil them until they can be mashed easily between your thumb and little finger. This will take about three hours. Then drain the beans and mash them while they are still hot. When they have cooled to 95–104°F, mix with the *koji* rice, and the salt, which should be combined together first.

Next, stuff the mixture into a keg or plastic bucket, smooth the surface, and rub a teaspoonful of salt into it. Place a sheet of plastic on top, then a lid cut to fit the surface area of the miso. Weigh this down with a weight of about six pounds. Finally, cover the container with brown wrapping paper or cut-up paper grocery bags, and tie it up with string.

Store the tub or bucket of developing miso in a cool, dark place. After a month, have a peek inside, but keep this brief to minimize the chances of unwanted microorganisms getting in. Check whether any liquid has formed on the surface of the miso. If it hasn't, you need to increase the weight pressing down on the lid. If and when the liquid has appeared, give the paste a mix, bringing the bottom to the top and vice versa. Reseal the container and mix again after another month. Then leave the miso in peace to mature.

After several months, the miso will start to smell good and turn yellow or light brown. You can try it after six months and it will keep improving for up to 18 months.

COOKING WITH MISO

Miso can be used to make delicious dressings, but it is most important as a basis for soups. Miso soup is a cornerstone of Japanese culture. Every household has its own take on the subject and new brides are expected to ditch the techniques they learned at home and replace them with those of their husbands' families.

· Miso soup is light, rich, and nutritious, and very easy to make. It is also extremely versatile.

MISO SOUP WITH PORK AND NOODLES

A simple miso soup is an essential component of a traditional Japanese breakfast, but more elaborate versions can be meals in themselves. This robust rural recipe is a good example, yielding a warming and filling soup. Serves 4

5 cups dashi—you can buy instant dashi in oriental food stores or make your own (see below)

7 ounces dried soba noodles

1 small white radish, cut into very thin strips

4 ounces carrots, cut into very thin strips (about 1–1½ cups)

4 ounces miso paste— about ½ cup (see left)

2 tablespoons soy sauce

2 tablespoons mirin

9 ounces pork tenderloin, sliced very thinly—about 1–1½ cups (the pork will be easier to slice paper thin if you half freeze it first)

4 scallions, chopped

- To make your own dashi (an important Japanese broth), get a six-inch piece of kombu (dried kelp) and one ounce of bonito flakes (¼–½ cupful), both available from Oriental and some "regular" supermarkets. Add to seven cups of water and simmer for 20 minutes. Do not let it come to a full boil. Let the flakes settle, then strain the liquid through a fine strainer and set aside. Alternatively, make up five cups of instant dashi according to the package instructions.
- Cook and drain the noodles according to the instructions on the package. Refresh with cold water and set aside.
- Heat the dashi in a large pot, add the radish and carrots, and simmer for five minutes.
- Add the miso to the soup and stir in thoroughly.
- Season the soup with the soy sauce and mirin, add the thinly sliced pork, and simmer for a few minutes until cooked.
- Serve in bowls with the noodles. Garnish with scallions.

BLACK BEAN SAUCE

With the exception of water and a little salt, black soybeans contain everything the human body needs. Their protein content rivals that of meat, but soy protein is much easier to digest. They are also about 11 percent carbohydrate and yield the world's number one cooking oil. The soybean, which provides tofu, miso, milk, soy sauce, and a good deal besides, has justifiably been called "the cow of China." Here we see what happens when you ferment it.

This dark, subtly hot sauce is fantastic with fish, as Chinese take-out restaurants have discovered from here to Timbuktu. For a richer experience, you can test your preserving patience and make black bean sauce yourself. Or you can cheat a little, saving a couple of years by buying ready-fermented beans from an Oriental grocery store. They are pungent and very salty, so you may want to rinse them before using them.

TO FERMENT BLACK BEANS

    2¼ pounds black soy beans
    10½ ounces salt (about 1 heaped cup)
    1 ounce ginger, peeled and roughly chopped
       (about 2 tablepoons)
    6 cloves of garlic, roughly chopped
    zest of 2 oranges

Soak the beans overnight, then parboil them for about 30 minutes.

Drain them, let them cool, then mix them with the remaining ingredients.

Pack the mixture tightly into sterilized jars and seal according to the instructions on page 164. Store at ambient temperature (for instance, in a pantry or cellar) for one to two years before use.

THE SAUCE—ENOUGH TO FILL ONE SMALL JAR

    1½ tablespoons fermented black beans (see above)
    2 teaspoons finely chopped garlic
    2 teaspoons finely chopped ginger
    ½ teaspoon finely chopped red chile
    1 tablespoon sesame oil
    2 teaspoons rice vinegar
    1½ teaspoons sugar
    1 star anise
    ⅔ cup chicken or pork broth
    1 tablespoon dark soy sauce
    1 sprig of cilantro, roughly chopped
    3 scallions, finely sliced
    1 teaspoon cornstarch mixed with 2 tablespoons
       water

Dip the black beans in a little warm water to take the salty edge off them, lifting them out with a slotted spoon.

Gently fry the garlic, ginger, and chile in the sesame oil for a couple of minutes.

Add the vinegar, sugar, star anise, and black beans, and simmer for a few more minutes.

Now add the chicken or pork broth and soy sauce, and cook gently for five minutes. Then add the cilantro and scallions.

Finally, making sure that the cornstarch is mixed well with the water, whisk it into the hot sauce. It should thicken immediately.

Spoon the sauce into a sterilized airtight container (see page 164). It will keep in the fridge for up to one week.

For a simple, satisfying dish, serve the black bean sauce with charbroiled salmon and rice.

SWEET CHILE RIBS WITH BLACK BEAN SAUCE

The fiery quality of black bean sauce is well suited to spare ribs, particularly if you have some sweet chile sauce to hand. This seems to douse the fire somewhat, even if technically it ought to enhance it. **Serves 4**

THE RIBS
24 pork ribs
4 cups chicken broth
1 small block of fresh
** ginger**
2 cloves of garlic
2 star anise
½ teaspoon five-spice
** powder**
A dash of soy sauce

THE SWEET CHILE SAUCE
See page 177

THE BLACK BEAN SAUCE
See page 150

- Simmer the ribs in the chicken broth, ginger, garlic, star anise, five-spice powder, and soy sauce for two hours. If the chicken broth fails to cover the ribs, top up with water.
- Coat the ribs in a little oil and about two-thirds cup of the sweet chile sauce. Either bake in the oven at 450°F for 10 minutes or grill on the barbecue. They won't take long as they are already cooked.
- Serve with the black bean sauce. A little goes a long way.

SUGAR

It may seem bizarre to us, in a world saturated with sugar and suffering

from it, that when "rock honey" first arrived in Europe in the early

Middle Ages, it was considered an incredibly healthy substance. There

were three main reasons. First, sugar fitted neatly into the prevailing

system of medicine. Secondly, it had remarkable preservative powers.

And finally, it was wildly expensive, so only a few monarchs were in danger of consuming too much. As late as the fifteenth century, by which time supply had expanded considerably, a teaspoon of sugar was worth £3 sterling in modern terms (or $5.25 if the dollar to pound exchange rate is 1.75).

The feature of sugar to leave the deepest impression on the medieval mind was its ability to preserve foods with which it had been coated or impregnated. We now understand this in terms of sucrose depriving bacteria of the chance to proliferate by forming air-tight barriers and sucking up moisture. Sugar is pure carbohydrate, so although the body can use it as a source of energy, a person living on nothing else would eventually die of malnutrition, not to say thirst. Similarly, microbes cannot survive in a pure sugar environment. But all this was a mystery to contemporary alchemists and proto-scientists. Nostradamus (1503–1566) was among those fascinated by this protean substance, which assumed several distinct forms (sticky, clear, brittle, smooth, opaque, grainy, etc.) depending on the temperature to which a sugar solution was boiled and the speed with which it was cooled. It comes as a surprise to realize that the supposed great seer of the future spent much of his time writing treatises on jam.

As far as equipment is concerned, a heavy pot will prove indispensable. This will help prevent burning, the curse of many a jam-maker. The pot will need to be tall enough to prevent sugar solutions from boiling over, have sloping sides to facilitate evaporation, and probably feature a lip to enable easy pouring. The other essential piece of equipment is a candy thermometer, which you may already possess if you're already addicted to home-smoking. This will allow you to precisely gauge what is known in the trade as the "height" to which you boil your sugar. This is vital if you are going to produce end products with the desired consistency. You don't want chutneys as brittle as glass or tasting of caramel.

To illustrate the need for precision, here is the list of thirteen "heights" of sugar boiling identified by Frederick Bishop in 1850. They are, in ascending order of the temperature to which sugar solutions must be boiled to produce them, *petit lissé* (equating to "smooth" in the English system), *lissé*, *petit perlé* (equating to "thread"), *grand perlé*, *petit queue de cochon* ("little pig's tail"), *grand queue de cochon* ("big pig's tail"), *soufflé*, *petit plume*, *grand plume* (the last two are described as "feather" by English sugar boilers), *petit boulet*, *grand boulet* (or "ball"), *cassé* (which produces a ball which will crumble and stick to the teeth when bitten) and finally *caramel*, which snaps clean when broken.

CARAMELIZED ALMOND CLUSTERS

We were faced with a dilemma here. Should we try to tackle the traditional smooth sugared almond long associated with weddings? In the end we decided not. Making such "comfits" demands specialty equipment and lots of time. A tilting "balancing pan" is needed to allow manipulation of the sugar syrup, which must be heated to exactly 216°F. Then the nuts are added and turned over constantly so that the syrup alternately coats them and dries to a hard shell. Several days and thousands of layers later, you have authentic sugared almonds.

It's a big task to do all this at home, so we've decided to show you a quicker method of preserving almonds in sugar. For caramelization, the syrup must be heated to "crack height" (310–315°F), a whisker beneath its scorching point. This requires care and precision.

TO MAKE ALMOND CLUSTERS

You need two pieces of special equipment to make this treat. The first is a silicon mat. Heatproof, flexible, and non-stick, these are the modern equivalents of the cold marble slabs traditionally used by confectioners to cool their wares. The next compulsory item is a thick-bottomed pan. It should have a heavy bottom which transfers heat evenly and responds quickly to temperature adjustments. This will give you the vital degree of control for this and several other sugar preserving processes.

> 1¼ pounds superfine sugar (about 3 cups)
> 11 ounces almonds, unskinned and unblanched
>   (about 2–2¾ cups)

Spread the almonds on a baking sheet and start heating them in a 300°F oven. Meanwhile, pour the sugar into your heavy pan and heat it slowly. Peer into the depths where the sugar meets the bottom of the pan and check that the sugar is clear as it melts—if it's dark, you're heating it too quickly. Stir the melting sugar gently. Clumps will form but as the minutes pass, the clumps will become smaller and smaller, until the sugar has completely melted.

When the sugar has melted, take the hot almonds out of the oven and add them to the sugar immediately—it's important you do this while the nuts are still hot. If the nuts were cold, the temperature of the syrup around them would drop briefly but significantly. Sugar crystals would start to form. If these precipitate in a big way in a hot syrup, you are in trouble. A chain reaction can set in, turning the whole batch grainy and leaving you with what seventeenth-century confectioners referred to as "sugar boil'd to sugar."

The sugar may coagulate again a bit anyway, but be patient and keep stirring. After five minutes or so, it will have smoothed out again. At this stage, you will hear the almonds "cracking" as they toast in the hot syrup. The sugar should have darkened to a smoky amber. If it remains clear, turn the heat up a tiny notch.

Now pour the molten conglomerate out onto the silicon mat and let cool until brittle. This will take 25 minutes or so. Break it into chunks and store it in a cool place in a cookie tin or packed into cellophane bags. Eat within two to three months.

CANDIED ORANGE PEEL

Although sugar cane was probably originally cultivated in New Guinea, it was the Indians, several thousand years ago, who worked out how to isolate crystalline sugar. The Sanskrit word for the pleasing nuggets thus produced was *khanda*, hence the English term "candy."

To the professional confectioner, "candy" means sugar boiled in a solution, then allowed or encouraged to recrystallize. As we mentioned in the instructions for making almond clusters, this can happen at the drop of a hat. Because recrystallization was so easy to arrange, the earliest sweet treats were invariably candied ones.

"Candying," when applied to fruit, means to soak it in syrup until most of its natural juices have been replaced by sugar via osmosis. This helps it to keep its shape and greatly increases its lifespan. In this sense, candied fruits are a kind of fossil. It's just that they have been infiltrated by a particularly appealing mineral.

TO MAKE CANDIED PEEL

Candying can transform things you wouldn't normally want to eat—in this case bitter orange peel—into luxurious delights. Try dipping one end of the finished peel in molten dark chocolate and the other in granulated sugar.

One of the ingredients here is glucose syrup. This is frequently used in the confectionary trade as a "doctor" to hinder recrystallization. Its function here is to give the candied orange peel luster and to prevent its surfaces from hardening.

> 2¼ pounds navel orange skin* (this equates to
> 9–11 pounds whole oranges)
> 4 pounds superfine sugar (about 8 cups)
> 1 cup glucose syrup, or corn syrup

*Try to get hold of unwaxed oranges. To skin them, cut into quarters and gently peel away the flesh. Alternatively, peel them whole and use the fruit to make Oranges in Brandy (page 184).

Cut the skin into strips and simmer them in water for about 30 minutes until soft. Drain the strips, then place them in a saucepan along with five cups of the sugar. Cover with water so that none of the peel is protruding, then simmer for half an hour. Remove the syrup from the heat and let cool with the saucepan lid on.

Next day, remove the strips of peel with a slotted spoon and set aside, then add one cup of sugar to the syrup and heat it to boiling point, making sure that all the "new" sugar dissolves. Remove the syrup from the heat, add the already cooked peel, then let the pan cool for another 24 hours, again with its lid on.

Repeat the process three more times, adding a cup of sugar to the syrup on each occasion until you have used it all up. On the fifth day, you add the glucose syrup instead. Bring to a boil as before, then pour the syrup over the peel.

Leave the peel covered for 24 hours, then remove it and lay it out on waxed paper. Let it dry for 24–48 hours until all moisture has disappeared but the peel is still soft.

Dip in them granulated sugar and store between layers of waxed paper in an airtight container for up to six months.

CANDIED ORANGE SEGMENTS

You can also candy entire orange segments in this way, with the skin still attached to the flesh. Proceed exactly as above, simmering the segments for a time before combining them with sugar. When ready, they are wonderful dipped in chocolate.

MARRONS GLACÉS

Chestnuts are pretty good anyway, with their melting, sweet-savory flesh, but steeping them in syrup transforms them into genuine delicacies. During their immersion, sugar penetrates them to the core, then starts to recrystallize. This takes place at a particular depth and with a slightly different texture each time the temperature of the syrup is adjusted. This is what gives the marrons their sophisticated, complex consistency. Our method is positively crude compared to the traditional, sixteen-stage French technique, but it still produces delectable results.

TO MAKE MARRONS GLACÉS

English sweet chestnuts are often on the small side. You can use them to make excellent marrons glacés, but nuts from Italy, Spain, France, and elsewhere are larger and very tempting.

> 2¼ pounds large sweet chestnuts
> 2½ cups water (plus water for simmering
>   the chestnuts)
> 1¼ pounds granulated sugar
> 1 cup liquid glucose or corn syrup
> 2 teaspoons natural vanilla extract

Using a sharp knife, cut two or three long shallow slits in each chestnut.

Heat a pot of water to 185°F, add the sweet chestnuts, and simmer them at this temperature for half an hour. You don't want to boil them as this would harden them.

Remove the pot from the heat and, as soon as the chestnuts are cool enough to handle, peel them one by one. You need to remove the outer shells but also the inner membranes. Use a paring knife and be very careful. If some of the nuts disintegrate, never mind.

If you are lucky, you will now have 30–40 pristine chestnuts. Place them in a single layer on a shallow, heat-resistant dish. Now combine the sugar and the water in a pan and boil until the temperature reaches 220°F. Pour the syrup over the chestnuts and leave in a cool place for 24 hours.

The following day, drain the syrup back into a pan and heat it to 230°F, a few degrees higher than before. Pour it over the chestnuts and let them steep overnight again.

For the final stage, drain the syrup into a pan as before, but this time add the liquid glucose or corn syrup, and the natural vanilla extract. Heat to 240°F (softball), pour over the chestnuts and transfer them into a sterilized jar, and seal (see page 164).

These marrons will keep in a cool place for an eternity. Nick uses them to make luxurious chocolate brownies.

CRYSTALLIZED VIOLETS

During the Middle Ages, crystallized violets (and rose petals) were a popular tonic for sick royal children. They will be familiar to many people as the sparkly, vivid-blue nuggets that sit on top of violet creams in fancy boxes of chocolates. In southern France you can buy them by the bagful. They are crunchy and aromatic and the color alone is enough to perk anyone up.

The two best varieties for crystallizing purposes are the sweet violet (*Viola odorata*) and the even more fragrant Parma violet. The plants are readily available in garden centers. Stay clear of yellow cultivars, in case you are tempted. Making the finished article is almost laughably simple.

TO MAKE CRYSTALLIZED VIOLETS
  20 fresh undamaged violet flowers, including a length of stalk (this is important for dipping purposes)
  1 egg white, whipped until frothy but not stiff
  1 tablespoon confectioners' sugar

Pick up a violet by the stalk and dip it into the egg white, or paint on the white with a brush. Gently shake off the excess egg, then sift confectioners' sugar over the flower while twirling it between your thumb and forefinger. The thin layer of sugar that adheres to the petals will be absorbed and form a crystalline crust.

Repeat the dipping and sugaring with all the violets, placing them on paper towels when done. Transfer them to the fridge, still sitting on the paper, and leave them there for a day. Then move them to a warm place and leave them for another 24 hours. The sugar should now have set.

At this stage you may want to separate the stems from the petals and discard them, as their work is done.

The crystallized flowers will keep for eight weeks in an airtight container. Use them as decorations for cakes, puddings, and chocolates.

PUMPKIN AND MAPLE SPREAD

Pumpkins are tremendous items, but let's face it, they can be one of life's problems. They're enormous, won't fit in your fridge's vegetable compartment, and most families find themselves with more orange pulp than they know what to do with after carving the Halloween jack-o'-lanterns.

Behold the solution. Struck by an inspiration, Nick managed to cadge some maple syrup from his father's errant brother Reuben, last seen stowing himself away on a ship to Canada some 50 years ago, but since rumored to have become a maple magnate. The result is a magnificent amber spread, dark, rich, grainy, and earthy.

3¼ pounds pumpkin, peeled and roughly cut up
1¼ pounds maple syrup
10 ounces clear honey (about 1 cup)
A couple of cinnamon sticks (optional)

Gather together enough canning jars to hold a total of eight cups to the finished product. Immerse the jars and their lids in boiling water for 10 minutes, and leave them in the hot water until you need them.

In a heavy saucepan, gently heat all the ingredients. When the liquid starts to simmer, froth will develop on the surface. Skim this off with a ladle to keep the liquid clear.

Gently boil for about one and a half hours. The pumpkin will become translucent. If any further froth appears, skim immediately. At the end of the cooking, discard the cinnamon sticks if using.

At this point, you could simply decant the product, because pumpkin preserved in this way is delicious. But we tend to blend it because the result is more versatile.

Pour into the sterilized jars immediately and seal (see page 164). The spread should keep for at least six months.

WAYS TO USE IT INCLUDE:
a) spread on toast with lashings of butter.
b) eaten with toasted waffles and whipped cream.
c) combined with cream and eggs to make a delicious pie or tart filling.
d) eaten neat when feeling low.

PUMPKIN, MAPLE, AND RASPBERRY TART

The god of the hearth moves in strange ways. This recipe was triggered by a table-tennis accident, in which Johnny tripped over one of Nick's giant pumpkins and continued into the raspberry patch. Fearful of litigation and finding himself with a lot of soft fruit and orange-colored pulp on his hands, Nick devised this excellent tart to mollify him. **Makes two tarts, each serving 6**

THE "JAM"
See the instructions on
page 161

THE PASTRY DOUGH
3¾ cups "00" grade
all-purpose flour
1½ cups confectioners'
sugar
1 cup plus 2 tablespoons
butter (2¼ sticks)
1 medium egg, plus 2 egg
yolks
½ teaspoon natural vanilla
extract

THE FILLING (TO FILL
2 TART SHELLS)
1¼ cups heavy cream
4 medium eggs
8 yolks
2½ cups pumpkin and
maple spread
(see page 161)
6 ounces raspberries
(about 1 cup)

- To make the dough, first sift the flour and confectioners' sugar into a large bowl. Work in the butter with your fingers until the mixture is soft and crumbly.
- Combine the egg, egg yolks, and vanilla, then make a well in the flour and pour the mixture in. Gradually stir in the flour, taking a little more into the center with every rotation of the spoon.
- Loosely press the dough out and divide it into two balls. Cover with plastic wrap and leave in the fridge for 30 minutes before you want to use it.
- Preheat the oven to 375°F. Take two eight-inch, removable-bottomed, fluted tart pans, about one and a half inches high. Roll out the pastry dough and press it out into the tart pans, so that a little hangs over the lip. Weigh down the pie shell by cutting out a circle of parchment paper or foil, placing it on the uncooked pie shell, and putting some dried beans or legumes on top.

- Bake in the oven for 10 minutes, then remove the beans, trim the crust with a sharp knife, and cook for another 15 minutes or until golden.
- To make the filling, whisk the cream, eggs, egg yolks, and pumpkin and maple spread together with an egg beater for 30 seconds, then add the raspberries.
- The best way to get the filling into the shells is to spoon it in while the shells are still resting on the oven shelf. Fill them to within a quarter-inch of the top and bake for one hour at 300–325°F. Check the tarts after 45 minutes. You should see the filling start to set from the sides inwards. As soon as this process is complete, the tarts are ready.

MANGO CHUTNEY

Mango chutney is so ubiquitous in the UK that people fail to appreciate how exotic it is. *Chatni*, which translates approximately to "finger licking," was originally an Indian relish made from fresh fruits and spices. British colonists picked up a taste for these "chutneys," brought them back to Europe, and adapted the recipes. Then they spread the habit throughout the Empire.

Good chutneys can be built around peaches, bananas, apricots, plums, cucumbers, apples, damson plums, or tomatoes, but the mother of them all has to be the mango. It is almost unthinkable to eat curry without it, and cheeseboards always benefit from its presence.

TO MAKE CHUTNEY
Traditional mango chutney is made with salted, pickled, green mangoes. These are not easy to obtain, however, so we use firm yellow mangoes instead. They make for a sweeter, better-colored chutney.

> 2¼ pounds mangoes, cut-up
> 2 ounces fresh ginger, peeled and cut into a fine julienne (about ¼ cup)
> 2 ounces medium-strength red chiles, seeds removed, cut into a fine julienne (about ⅓ cup)
> 1 cup cider vinegar
> 1 cup light brown sugar

Place all the ingredients in a pot and bring to a boil. Simmer for one hour, then pack into sterilized containers and seal (see page 164) and store in a cool place for up to one year.

QUINCE CHEESE

This is no more a cheese than apple butter is butter, but it does have a texture similar to cream cheese. In fact, its scented, honey-like flavor goes very well with cream cheese. It is also delicious with cold meats or foie gras. As it ages, quince cheese becomes firmer, darker, and more intense in flavor.

4½ pounds quinces
Juice of 1 lemon
Sugar, equal in volume to the quince flesh after
coring and peeling

Core and peel the quinces, reserving the flesh. Heat the cores and peelings in a pot along with one cup water and simmer for an hour. Put the pulp through a food mill or conical perforated sieve with pestle, and reserve.

Weigh the quince flesh, then place it in a thick-bottomed pot with the sieved pulp, lemon juice, and another cup of water, and simmer for one hour.

Blend the pulp with an immersion blender or food processor until smooth.

Measure the pulp and add the sugar, cup for cup. Slowly cook the purée for another two hours, stirring occasionally, until it has darkened to a deep rose. The cheese is ready when it is so thick that a spoon drawn across the bottom of the pan leaves a definite path in its wake.

Lightly grease a shallow, non-stick, baking tray and pour the cheese in to a depth of about one and a quarter inches. Let it set overnight, then turn it out onto a length of cheesecloth and wrap the fabric around it. Then fold a couple of sheets of newspaper over the whole lot and store in a dark place for one month before eating. The quince cheese will keep for up to one year.

LEMON CURD

A good lemon curd is fresh tasting and packed with the essence of the fruit. The richness of the ingredients means that it only has a limited shelf-life, but we're still talking six weeks in the fridge if properly sealed.

Homemade lemon curd is invariably nicer than the store-bought equivalent. It is excellent on toast and, of course, in lemon meringue pies. For many, eating curd made according to this recipe is like stumbling on a long-forgotten treasure.

4 large or 5 medium lemons, zested and juiced
(use unwaxed lemons, and large juicy ones at that)
4 large eggs
1¾ cups superfine sugar
1 cup plus 2 tablespoons (2¼ sticks) unsalted
butter, cut into small cubes
1 level tablespoon cornstarch
3 x 1¼-cup jars
3 wax discs to fit the mouth of the jars (available
from jam and catering stores)

Sterilize the jars (see page 164) and keep them at hand along with the wax discs.

Pour all the ingredients into a saucepan and whisk vigorously for 30 seconds.

Heat over a low flame, whisking constantly to make sure the contents don't stick to the side of the pan. A food thermometer is useful here. The mixture hitting 158°F is a sign that the eggs and cornstarch are about to emulsify and gelatinize.

Once the mixture has thickened, continue cooking for just another minute, then remove the pan from the heat.

Pour the curd into the jars through a funnel. Lay the wax discs over the tops, then seal (see page 164). Let cool, then store in the fridge for up to six weeks.

LEMON MERINGUE PIE

A good lemon meringue pie is a lovesome thing, but as life sadly teaches us, there is plenty of scope for messing it up. Institutions of all kinds, from schools to office canteens, are masters at ruining them. Bland, over-sweet or suspiciously colored curd is adorned with unset, soapy meringue. This may be why the pleasure is so deep when you eat an authentic, homemade L.M.P. **Makes 2 tarts, each serving 4–6**

THE PASTRY DOUGH

3¾ cups "00" grade all-purpose flour

1½ cups confectioners' sugar

Zest of 1 lemon

1 cup plus 2 tablespoons (2¼ sticks) butter

1 medium egg, plus 2 egg yolks

½ teaspoon natural vanilla extract

THE MERINGUE AND FINAL TOUCHES

4 medium egg whites, plus 3 egg yolk

½ cup superfine sugar

¼ cup heavy cream

2 cups lemon curd (see page 171)

⅔ cup confectioners' sugar

- Make the curd according to the instructions on page 171, or grab a jar from the fridge.
- To make the dough, first sift the flour and confectioners' sugar into a large bowl. Add the lemon zest, then work in the butter with your fingers until soft and crumbly.
- Mix the eggs, egg yolks, and vanilla together, make a well in the flour, then stir the egg mixture into it.
- Press the pastry dough out loosely, then divide into two balls. Cover in plastic wrap and let rest in the fridge for 30 minutes before use.
- Preheat the oven to 375°F.
- Take two eight-inch, removable-bottomed, fluted tart pans about an inch high. Roll out the dough and press it into the tart pans, so that it hangs slightly over the lip. Weigh it down by cutting out circles of parchment paper or foil, placing them on the uncooked pie shell and evenly placing dried beans or legumes on top.
- Bake in the oven for 10 minutes, then remove the dried beans, trim the crust with a sharp knife, and cook for another 15 minutes or until golden.

- To make the meringue topping, simply whisk the egg whites and sugar until the mixture forms stiff peaks. This is easily done with an electric beater. If you are doing it by hand, first beat the egg whites until stiff, then add and whisk in the sugar a little at a time. The mixture should become glossy.
- Now you must put the whole thing together. Stir the egg yolks and cream into the lemon curd. Sift in the confectioners' sugar and whisk it in. Then pour the whole mixture into the pie shells. Then cover the filling with the egg white and sugar foam. The easiest and neatest way to do this is through a piping bag, but if you don't have the equipment, just spoon on the meringue topping and smooth it with a plastic spatula or butter knife.
- Bake in the oven at 325°F for 40 minutes. The pies are ready when the meringue is crispy and slightly colored on top, and soft in the middle.

NICK'S MARMALADE

To those of us accustomed to the orange kind, or lime if we're feeling radical, it seems strange that marmalade was originally made from quinces. It takes its name from *marmelo*, the Portuguese word for quince. Significant quantities of "marmelada" were imported into Britain during the fifteenth century, but it was a couple of centuries later, when people started to make marmalade with bitter Seville oranges, that its popularity really soared.

The U.S.P. (unique selling point) of our marmalade is the fineness of its shreds. Nick is no big fan of large shards of peel in his marmalade, preferring tiny particles of zest lost in a golden expanse of jelly.

For this recipe you will need a very large pot with a capacity of around two and a half gallons. This is a lot of marmalade, but you'll find yourself giving most of it away to pleading friends and relatives.

TO FILL QUITE A FEW JARS:
- 11 pounds Seville oranges (if unavailable, use other bitter oranges)
- 7 lemons
- 2 quarts orange juice (in addition to the juice you squeeze out of the oranges)
- Water to top up
- Lots of sugar
- Lots of cheesecloth

Zest the oranges with a zester or use the finest face of a cheese-grater. This can be time consuming, but no more than the main alternative, which is to cut the peel into shreds. Spread the procedure over a couple of days if you like. The zest will keep in the fridge for up to four days.

Squeeze the lemons and scoop out their innards, pith, seeds and all. Discard the peel and reserve the rest.

Cut the oranges in half and squeeze the juice. Put all parts of them, except for the reserved zest, into the pot, adding the lemon juice, pith, and seeds. Press down the orange halves, then pour in the two quarts of orange juice. Top up with water until the liquid just seeps over the tops of the oranges.

Bring to a boil, then simmer for one hour with the lid on.

Remove the pot from the heat and let it cool. After 24 hours, return the marmalade to the heat and gently boil for two hours. Transfer the contents of the pan into the center of an extremely large square of cheesecloth. Squeeze and manipulate it to extract as much juice as possible.

Measure the collected juice and return it to a clean pot, adding an equal amount of sugar (one cup sugar for each cup of juice). Bring the juice back to a boil and now add the reserved zest. Keep boiling until the mixture has reached setting point (220°F). Carry out the setting test to reassure yourself that it will set (see page 164).

Funnel the marmalade into sterilized jars, then seal them (see page 164), and label them.

Store in a pantry or cupboard for up to one year.

ALCOHOL

Many of the world's favorite alcoholic drinks are made with fruits, so it

seems particularly appropriate to use it to preserve them. Alcohol is

itself a product of a preserving process (fermentation) and it in turn has

a powerful embalming effect on food immersed in it. Nothing can

grow in pure alcohol, which is why it is used by entomologists and botanists to keep biological specimens intact. For this reason, it is usually best to use the strongest available brand of the relevant liquor for preserving purposes.

There is more truth than you might think in the old story of the priest who decided to preach a sermon on the evils of booze. First he put an earthworm in a glass of water, where it wriggled about quite happily. Then he placed it in a tumbler of whisky. It dropped to the bottom stone dead. "And what is the lesson here?" he asked his congregation. "I know," shouted out an old drunk who had blundered into the church. "Water gives you worms."

In the Middle Ages, when water supplies were untreated, drinking "Adam's ale" (water) could pose a serious health hazard. In this context, brewing and distilling were not simply luxuries; they were also forms of hygiene. Even children were given "small beer." Monks were particularly expert at making alcohol and flavoring it with fruits and herbs. They also pioneered the practice of steeping the fruits they grew in their orchards in spirits and liqueurs to prolong their shelf-lives. The end-products were warming and cheering, especially in winter. They also occupied an important niche in the humoral system of medicine.

Fruits preserved in alcohol became so popular during the eighteenth century that many varieties, including peaches, apricots, cherries, and nectarines, went by the generic name of "brandy fruits." They were typically served in dedicated glasses at the end of indulgent Georgian meals.

When fruits are immersed in alcohol, they absorb its flavors and vice versa. The sugars they contain are also encouraged to ferment, particularly if extra sugar is added. This is the principle behind the manufacture of Sloe Gin (see opposite). Aside from the kick imparted, preserving fruits in alcohol has many advantages over other methods. There is no need to use additives, no loss of vitamins through heat treatment, and the fruit stays firm. The results are also beautiful and go very well with ice cream.

SLOE GIN

Sloes, the fruit of the spiky blackthorn bush, grow wild along many paths and hedgerows in the UK. They ripen in the autumn and are like hard, miniature, vividly blue plums, to which they are closely related. Sloes impart a wonderful, warming fruitiness and color to gin or vodka. You wouldn't want to eat them raw as they are far too bitter, but numerous birds think otherwise. You will be in direct competition with them for the harvest.

Tradition has it that the best time to pick sloes is after the first frost of autumn has swollen and softened them slightly. You might want to wear gloves as blackthorns are notoriously prickly.

TO MAKE ENOUGH TO SEE YOU THROUGH TO THE FOLLOWING AUTUMN
     4½ pounds sloes (a good afternoon's harvest)
     2¼ pounds sugar (about 5–5¼ cups)
     3 bottles of gin or vodka, the higher proof, the better

The onerous part is pricking each fruit several times with a needle, or, more traditionally, a blackthorn spike. Either way, settle down for a couple of meditative hours. Place the pricked sloes in a large sealable jar, pour in the sugar, then add the alcohol. Seal the jar and turn it upsidedown several times to distribute the sugar and start it dissolving.

Let the gin/vodka mature in a cool, dark place for six months. Turn it over occasionally, particularly in the early stages.

After this period, strain the liquid through cheesecloth or clean cotton cloth and decant it into sterilized bottles (see page 164). If you're smart, you will have kept the original liquor bottles and their caps. Wait six months to one year before drinking.

MORELLO CHERRIES IN KIRSCH

The dark morello cherries that grow in abundance in the Black Forest in Germany are too sour to simply eat from the tree. Instead, the locals mash them in large wooden tubs and let them ferment. The end result is *kirsch* or *kirschwasser*, a dry, colorless hooch with quite a kick to it. Fresh cherries steeped in the kirsch become eminently edible. Their sourness is replaced by a luxurious tangy sweetness, and they are immediately co-opted into a *Schwarzwalderkirchtorte* (Black Forest cake).

> **2¼ pounds morello cherries**
> **1¾ cups sugar**
> **1¼ cups water**
> **⅔ cup brandy**
> **⅔ cup kirsch**

Cut slits down the sides of the cherries with a paring knife, then ease out the pits. Alternatively, leave the pits in, but cut a cross in each cherry at the stalk end to let the juices out and the alcohol in.

Put a half-cup of the sugar along with all of the water in a pan and bring to a boil. Add the cherries and simmer for five minutes.

Remove the cherries with a slotted spoon and set aside. Add the rest of the sugar to the syrup, dissolve, and boil gently for five minutes. Let cool.

Drop the cherries into a sterilized canning jar (see page 164) until filled to the neck. Then combine the brandy and kirsch with the syrup and pour it in. Seal the jar (see page 164) and wait at least three months before use.

These cherries are the defining ingredient of the morello cherry trifle opposite.

TRIFLE WITH MORELLO CHERRIES

There isn't enough space here to fully extol the virtues of this trifle, but consider it the last word on the subject. **Serves 6**

THE CUSTARD
½ cup superfine sugar
2¾ cups whole milk
½ cup heavy cream
3 tablespoons cornstarch
1 teaspoon natural vanilla extract
Pinch of vanilla seeds
6 large egg yolks, lightly beaten

THE SPONGECAKE
⅔ cup (1¼ sticks) unsalted butter, softened
¾ cup superfine sugar
2 large eggs, plus 4 large egg yolks
Few drops of natural vanilla extract
2 cups "00" grade (extra fine) flour
2½ teaspoons baking powder
Large pinch of salt

½ cup milk
½ cup cream
9-inch cake pan with removable bottom

THE SYRUP AND THE CHERRIES
1½ cups jar morello cherries preserved in kirsch (see left)

THE TRIMMINGS
½ cup shelled pistachios, lightly roasted in the oven for 5 minutes at 375°F, then crushed
High-quality dark chocolate, for grating
1¾ cups heavy cream with 2 tablespoons sugar whipped in

6 glasses holding around a cup each

- Make the custard: combine the sugar, milk, cream, cornstarch, vanilla extract, and vanilla seeds in a thick-bottomed saucepan. Simmer for five minutes, whisking continuously.
- Remove from the heat and whisk in the egg yolks.
- Return to a very low heat for a minute or two, then the custard will be ready. Store it in the fridge until you need it.
- Butter the bottom and sides of the cake pan, then sift flour over the whole buttered area to create a non-stick barrier.
- Preheat the oven to 350–375°F.
- Cream the butter, preferably with an electric beater, until lightened in color. Then add the sugar and continue to beat for four to five minutes. You may need to switch the beater off from time to time and fold the mixture in with a spatula.
- Slowly add the eggs. If you do this too fast, the mixture will curdle. Then add the vanilla extract.
- Combine the flour with the baking powder and salt. Add a little of the dry mixture to the butter, sugar, and eggs, then add a little of the milk and cream. Keep alternating dry and wet ingredients until they have all been incorporated.
- Stir the mixture until smooth. Then pour it into the cake pan and bake for 30–40 minutes. If the surface of the sponge starts to brown during cooking, turn the heat down a little. To check whether the cake is ready, insert a toothpick into the center. If it comes out clean, it's done.
- Push the cake out of the pan and onto a cake rack to cool. You will have too much for this recipe, so freeze the rest.
- Pour the kirsch syrup into a pan, reserving the cherries and, reduce by half over medium heat. Reserve and chill, along with the roughly chopped cherries.
- Slice the cake into layers about an inch thick, then cut it to fit your glasses. Pour over the reduced kirsch syrup, then fill each glass in the following order: cherries, custard, pistachios, spongecake, then the same again, then a dollop of cream. Shave or grate a little chocolate on the summit.

ORANGES IN BRANDY

Brandy-soaked oranges were a big hit at bibulous Georgian dinner parties. Oranges were still something of rarity, which gave them status and, given their limited lifespan, it made good sense to preserve them. Guests were not disappointed when they found that the juice in each segment had swapped place with the fragrant alcohol. The beauty of this dish lies in the trick it plays on the brain. The orange looks freshly cut but tastes wonderfully boozy. Each mouthful comes as a surprise to the tastebuds, even when you've consciously gotten the hang of the situation.

These oranges make beautiful gifts, packed tightly in their deep amber cosmoses. To vary both visual effect and flavor, try experimenting with blood oranges, ortaniques, mandarins, or whatever orange citrus takes your fancy.

HOW TO MAKE ORANGES ALCOHOLIC

12 small oranges
1¾ cups sugar
1¼ cups water
1¼ cups brandy
2 canning jars around 1 quart each in capacity

Remove the zest from the oranges with a grater. Simmer the zest in some water for 30 seconds, then drain and set aside.

Peel the oranges, cutting into the flesh to make the globes slightly smaller than they otherwise would be. The individual sacs of juice inside the segments should be exposed.

Heat the sugar and water in a saucepan, making sure that all the sugar dissolves. Simmer the oranges in the syrup for two minutes, then remove. Boil the syrup for five more minutes, then remove from the heat and let cool.

Pack the oranges up to the necks of the sterilized jars (see page 164), adding a few sprinkles of the reserved zest.

Stir the brandy into the syrup, then pour the liquid into the jars, making sure the oranges are completely covered.

Seal the jars (see page 164) and let them mature in a cool dark place for a minimum of two months. Once opened, they will keep for six months as long as the oranges are covered by liquid.

A BOOZY ORANGE DESSERT

Nick has devised a fine dessert based on oranges in brandy. To make enough for four people, cut four of the preserved oranges into segments and reduce their preserving liquid until quite viscous (about a quarter of its initial volume). Meanwhile, cook eight fresh, dark plums in ¼ cup port and ¼ cup of sugar. Put them through a food mill, reserving the juice. Arrange all the ingredients in flute glasses interspersed with scoops of vanilla ice cream. Pour the liquids on top and garnish with a little zest.

LAI'S FRUITS-OF-THE-FOREST-FLAVORED RUM

There are several long, thin bottles under Nick's stairs, laid down horizontally and covered in foil. They were put there seven years ago by his now-wife Lai when she was marking out her territory. Inside them lies the nectar of the gods. Occasionally, if they have had a baby or won the lottery or similar, they decant a nip or two and luxuriate in its beneficial properties. This is a welcome release from their frugal lifestyle.

Nick has been nagging Lai for the recipe for seven years. Only her sense of duty to this book made her relent. She sighed deeply and revealed her secret, "I went to Marks & Spencer, bought loads of frozen 'fruits-of-the-forest' mix, stuffed it into rum bottles, and then topped it up with rum and sugar." All the mystery has now gone out of their marriage.

Bear in mind that it is the liquid we are interested in here, not the fruit mush, which you are under no compulsion to eat.

2¼ pounds frozen fruits-of-the-forest mix*
1½ cups sugar
4 cups dark rum
Aluminum foil to wrap the bottles
3 used 750ml liquor or liqueur bottles with their original corks or caps

*You can buy this from supermarkets, or you can collect your own fruits and freeze them, taking a look at Chapter 12 *en route*. Good fruits to use include black currants, red currants, blueberries, blackberries, strawberries, and raspberries.

Patiently insert the fruits-of-the-forest into the sterilized bottles (see page 164).

Mix the sugar with the rum and decant into the bottles via a sterilized funnel.

Cover the bottles with foil and leave for at least a year. It doesn't hurt to give them a little shake from time to time.

Serve neat, or try in a cocktail with champagne and fresh blackberries.

BOTTLING AND CANNING

If one invention has been more responsible than any other for the spectacular increase in the human population over the last few centuries, it is that of the microscope. Prior to this breakthrough, the true cause of the majority of diseases was anyone's guess. And this, of course, applied to food poisoning.

CASSOULET

Nick can make this in his sleep and, on occasion, he has had to. There was a time, during our brief but glorious career as soup tycoons, when half the West End of London ate this cassoulet every lunchtime. Or that's how it seemed. We didn't used to can it, but we easily could have, and with hindsight, we probably should have.

This recipe produces a tasty, warming, and satisfying soup/stew which takes very close to life in a jar.

5 cups pork or chicken broth
1¼ pounds dried lima beans (about 3 cups)
1 duck breast
2¼ pounds Toulouse sausage (or "Taplows,"
   see page 92)
1 carrot, cut-up
2 stalks of celery, cut-up
1 small onion, chopped fine
¼ cup pancetta, finely chopped (see page 70)
2 tablespoons all-purpose flour
1 cup tomato puree (see page 195)
4 bay leaves
A couple of sprigs of thyme
Salt and pepper

We make our broth from the spare ribs and skin of the pork belly that we use for sausages. You could also use chicken broth if you like. The fat should be skimmed from the broth and reserved.

Soak the dried beans overnight, then simmer for one and a half hours hours or until soft.

Either hot-smoke the duck breast (see page 76) for one hour at 230°F or pan-fry for five minutes on each side, reserving the oil Cut up the breast meat when cool.

Fry the sausages until lightly browned, then thickly slice when cool. Reserve all fat and juices.

Heat the pork stock in a small pan.

Take the reserved oils amassed during the preparation of this dish and pour a third-cupful into a large saucepan. Fry the carrot, celery, onion, and pancetta in the oil over medium heat for around 10 minutes or until soft.

Add the flour and stir in until it has soaked up all the fat. Then add the tomato puree, mixing it in well to remove any lumps. Slowly add the hot stock, stirring vigorously as you go, until it is all incorporated. Add the sausage, duck, cooked beans, bay leaves, and thyme. Simmer for half an hour, then season with salt and pepper to taste. This dish needs to be stirred frequently while cooking because the flour it contains is liable to stick.

PRESSURE CANNING
You can either hot- or raw-pack the cassoulet. We'd recommend hot. Leave a gap of an inch between the surface of the stew and the lid of the jar. Process the cassoulet in your canner for 75 minutes if packed into pint jars, and 90 minutes if in quart jars. The pressure settings should be as follows, depending on your altitude:

Sea level—2,000 feet – 0.76 bar/11 p.s.i.
2,000–4,000 feet – 0.83 bar/12 p.s.i.
4,000–6,000 feet – 0.9 bar/13 p.s.i.
6,000–8,000 feet – 0.97 bar/14 p.s.i.

Leave to cool at room temperature and store for up to one year.

AIR EXCLUSION

Successful food preservation has two elements. The first is the killing or dramatic suppression of potentially harmful organisms present in the food itself. This is the primary purpose of all the drying, salting, smoking, pickling, boiling, and fermenting we have encountered in previous chapters. But the next line of defense is to prevent dubious microbes getting at the food in the first place—or the second if something has been done to it to kill off the nasties in round one. This applies to all the items in this chapter, even if all that has happened to them is a period of cooking.

The simplest and most ancient technique of putting up a barrier against airborne organisms is to pack the relevant food in some (preferably edible) substance, such as butter, that the airborne organisms are unable to get their teeth into. Not so much, as it turns out, because the airborne organisms find the butter or other fats typically employed inedible, but because most of the microbes are killed during the cooking phase, and the rest are unable to get in, or to move and hence breed, once the fat has congealed. This is the rationale behind the layer of butter on top of a delicate pâté, or the creamy duck fat in which *confit de canard* is entombed. The most beautiful dishes preserved in this way are those relying on clear mediums such as aspic, which holds the food in highly visible suspended animation.

One of the oldest preserved foods relying on the principle of air exclusion is Lebanese *qawrama*. This is a kind of *confit* made from the browned, lean meat of the so-called fat-tailed sheep. This meat is combined with rendered fat from that animal's abundant tail and sealed in special canning jars. Fat-tailed sheep were already well established in Arabia by the middle of the first millennium B.C.E. Amazed Greek authors reported that the appendages that gave them their name were sometimes so large that they had to be supported by little carts.

In Britain, potted meats became all the rage during the late seventeenth century, once the technology was in place to mass-produce suitable vessels. All kinds of seafood and game were preserved in this manner, as were domestic products like pork and beef. The food was liberally spiced with pepper, nutmeg, and cloves, and packed into earthenware tubs sealed with clarified butter or pork or duck fat. These potted products were the forefathers of the soft pastes, like deviled ham, that today fill the sandwiches of a million small children. Some would keep for several months.

The other way, of course, of preventing airborne microbes getting at your food is to surround it with literally nothing. Vacuum packing may lack the glamour of the venerable methods covered elsewhere in this book, but for keeping preserved items in pristine condition, it is unrivaled.

VACUUM PACKING

If food is encased in a plastic wrapper molded to fit its contours, airborne organisms will be unable to get in and aerobic organisms inside will be denied the oxygen they need to function. Vacuum packing is commonly used in the catering industry for preserving purposes. In essence, it works like this: the food is placed between two sheets of plastic and these are sealed together on three ends with hot pressing irons. This makes a "bag," out of which the air is then sucked with a pump. Then the fourth end of the "bag" is sealed before air has a chance to get back in.

Vacuum packing is eminently feasible in the home and it will greatly enhance your preserving options. Food packaged in this way will keep in the fridge for at least twice as long as usual. If it is frozen, the preserving effect is even more pronounced. Fish will keep for up to two years instead of the usual two to three months, and red meats for as long as five years. Oily foods will not become rancid or bitter tasting.

A new home vacuum packer will cost you a bit, but you may be able to find a decent second-hand one. The process is fun to watch. When the air is evacuated, the plastic suddenly clings to the food like a second skin.

ASPIC

As "preserved in aspic" is a common expression in everyday English, it would be foolish of us not to say something about it here. But we should point out that aspic on its own only preserves food very briefly (items canned in it are another matter). The familiar metaphor refers more to the undisturbed beauty of food preserved in aspic than to its longevity.

Aspic in its purest form is the clear, protein-rich jelly that forms under a cold roast chicken or a refrigerated ham. In practice, it is usually made from meat or fish stock. This is often reduced to ensure a better set, or gelatin is added to it. The outcome is a delicate savory jelly. Aspic makes an attractive glaze, helping to prevent the food it coats from drying out, and in larger quantities, it can hold morsels in apparent defiance of gravity.

Johnny's great-aunt, who brought him up, made the following appetizer every time she cooked a big meal. It looked as though it must have taken ages to make, but in fact was virtually instant. It went down so well that she never felt the need to deviate.

EGGS AND SHRIMP IN ASPIC (FOR EACH DINER)
A small handful of cooked peeled shrimp
A couple of chives, chopped
1 cup good tinned beef consommé
A dash of sherry
½ hardboiled egg
1 ramekin or custard cup

Mix the shrimp and chives with the consommé and sherry.

Fill the bottom third of each ramekin with the mixture and gently place the egg in it, curved side down. Then spoon the remaining consommé over it so that the egg is well covered. Smooth the surface with a spatula.

Chill and serve. For added effect, garnish each ramekin with a shrimp and a few lengths of chive.

CONFIT DE CANARD

This method of preserving duck legs and thighs in fat originates from southwest France. The meat is soft, dark, and intensely flavored. You may end up licking your plate.

Salt
6 duck legs
Cracked black pepper
3 cloves
2 cloves of garlic
1¾ pounds goose or duck fat, lard, olive oil,
   or a combination of all four (about 3½ cups)

Sprinkle salt onto the exposed flesh of each duck leg. Fold the legs together so the salted areas are touching and leave them in the fridge for 24 hours.

Wipe the legs down and firmly place them in an ovenproof dish with a tight-fitting lid, along with the pepper, cloves, and garlic.

Cook in the oven at 350°F for two and a half hours.

Let the legs cool in their own fat, then pack them tightly into sterilized jars (see page 164). Heat the additional fat/oil/lard (i.e., not that released by the duck) and when molten, pour it over the duck up to the necks of the jars. Seal (see page 164), store in the fridge, and eat within a fortnight.

GOOSE RILLETTES

The French are less uptight about fat than most nationalities. They recognize its role in a healthy diet and are careful to distinguish between good and bad kinds. Above all, they know that enjoying your food can put years on your life, offsetting any theoretical health risks. Jeanne Calment, the longest-lived human being of all time, didn't get to 122 years old on a diet of bean sprouts.

Rillettes consist of seasoned meat slowly cooked in fat, then teased apart and preserved in it.

1 goose, weighing around 9 pounds
1¾ pounds pork shoulder, boned
1¼ pounds pork belly fat
3 bay leaves
3 thyme sprigs
8 black peppercorns
Salt
6 juniper berries

Remove the skin from the goose. Bone the bird, then cut the meat into chunks, reserving any fat you come across.

Mince together the pork shoulder, belly fat, and goose fat.

Combine all the ingredients in a large, heavy-based pan. Cook slowly for three hours with the lid on, stirring occasionally. Don't let the mixture stick. If it starts to, add a drop or two of water.

The goose meat will eventually start to fall apart. You can hasten the process by teasing it with a fork.

Sterilize some jars (see page 164). Take out the goose meat with a slotted spoon and press it down firmly into them. Pour the remaining fat on top, cover, and let it set in the fridge.

Serve with warm French bread and cheap rosé wine. The rillettes will keep for at least two weeks in the fridge.

CHICKEN LIVER PATE WITH MORELS

This is as much about texture as taste, with nuggets of morel interrupting the luxurious smoothness.

- 10 medium-sized fresh morels, or any other good edible mushrooms
- ¾ cup plus 2 tablepoons (1¾ sticks) unsalted butter
- 14 ounces chicken livers (about 1¾ cups)— or duck if you prefer
- 2 cloves of garlic, finely chopped
- ¼ cup brandy
- 1 teaspoon mustard powder
- Salt and finely ground white pepper
- 1 sprig of thyme, finely chopped
- ½ teaspoon freshly grated nutmeg
- ¼ cup heavy cream
- A scant cup clarified butter (see "Potted Shrimp" on page 206)

Roughly chop the mushrooms and gently fry them in two tablespoons of the unsalted butter for five minutes.

Fry the liver and garlic in a quarter-cup unsalted butter over medium heat until cooked through. This will take 8–10 minutes.

Remove the livers with a slotted spoon and place them in a blender. Pour the brandy into the pan, swish it about in the remaining fat and juices, and pour all of it into the blender. Add the remaining butter to the pan, melt it, and put in the blender along with the mustard powder, salt, pepper, thyme, nutmeg, and cream.

Blend until smooth. Then pour into a mixing bowl. Toss in the mushrooms and mix with a spoon until evenly distributed.

Spoon the mixture into a sterilized earthenware dish (see page 164) and smooth the surface with a butter knife or plastic spatula. Leave the pâté in the fridge for an hour or so to set.

Heat the clarified butter and pour it over the pâté so that the surface is covered.

Cover and return to the fridge. This pâté will have a shelf-life of seven days in the fridge prior the seal being broken. After breaking the layer of clarified butter, consume within three days.

WILD MUSHROOM PATE

We'll finish with this nice vegetarian pâté, a prudent thing to make after a successful afternoon's foraging.

- 1 pound chanterelle or oyster mushrooms (about 4–5 cups), sliced
- ¼ cup (½ stick) butter
- 2 medium shallots, chopped
- 1–2 cloves of garlic, crushed
- 1 ounce dried porcini mushrooms (see page 21), cleaned but unsoaked
- 4 ounces dried green lentils (about ½ cup)
- ½ cup cream cheese
- ½ cup crème fraîche (if unavailable, use sour cream)
- Salt
- Cracked black pepper
- 1 sprig of flat-leaf parsley, chopped
- A scant cup clarified butter (see "Potted Shrimp" on page 206)

Fry the fresh mushrooms in the butter along with the shallots and garlic. They will release lots of juice. Gently cook until this has reduced by at least half.

Add the dried porcini to the lentils and just cover with water. Gently cook until all the water has been soaked up. Check the lentils to see if they are ready. If not, add a little more water and continue cooking until they are.

Add the lentils to the chestnut mushrooms and blend in a food processor until smooth.

Add the cream cheese, crème fraîche, salt, pepper, and chopped parsley.

Spoon the pâté into a suitable, sterilized container (see page 164). Warm the clarified butter and pour it over. Cover and leave to set in the fridge.

The pâté will keep for five days in the fridge. Once you've broken into the seal, consume within three days.

POTTED SHRIMP

After a bereavement, a kindly neighbor asked Johnny if she could do anything for him. "You wouldn't mind picking up some potted shrimp for me in town?" he replied.

Potted shrimp are very comforting. They are delicate, mildly spiced, and redolent of a bygone era. The crustaceans in question are the small, gray-to-brown kind caught with a shrimping net on old-style British seaside holidays. You can buy them ready-prepared, but this is expensive.

½ cup (1 stick) unsalted butter

¼ teaspoon cayenne pepper

2–3 blades of mace

A good grating of nutmeg

14 ounces cooked, peeled tiny shrimp
(about 2½–3 cups)

⅔ cup clarified butter*

*To clarify the butter, slowly melt it in a pan. Skim the scum from the surface, then ladle off the clear, clarified butter, and leave behind the watery residue which will have collected at the bottom of the pan. Pour the butter into a jar and store in the fridge.

Heat the unsalted butter in a pan until melted but not boiling. Add the cayenne pepper, mace, and nutmeg, and stir in.

Add the shrimp and gently cook for five minutes to re-sterilize them.

Scoop the shrimp and spiced butter into two one-and-a-half-cup-sized ramekins or custard cups (see page 164). Press them down to compact them.

Place in the fridge until set. This will take about 30 minutes.

Heat the clarified butter and pour it onto the shrimp. Once set, it will form an impermeable seal.

The shrimp will have a shelf-life of two weeks in the fridge as long as the butter seal remains intact, and three days once broken.

FREEZING

Secreted in the woodland near where Johnny lives is what looks like a

wildly overgrown stone igloo. Today it is only used by children playing

hide-and-seek or teenagers up to something less innocent. But it is,

in fact, a Victorian ice-house. Long before the invention of the

refrigerator, wealthy Europeans and Americans were building these edifices and filling them with ice brought by ship from the far north to enable them to chill food during the summer. Often their primary purpose was to meet the already insatiable demand for ice cream. But the Victorians were not the first to build ice-houses. The Mesopotamians were at it four thousand years ago, and the Egyptians, Greeks, Persians, and Chinese, none of whose summers was exactly cold, were not far behind. The Inuit, meanwhile, have been aware of the preservative powers of ice since before time began. Indeed, some families in the Arctic have been known to use refrigerators to *prevent* their food from freezing, as the fridges keep their food a couple of degrees above 32°F. Similarly, residents of the altoplano in the Andes have been freeze-drying potatoes for eons. They crush their spuds and spread them on rocks at altitudes in excess of 15,000 feet. At night, when the temperature falls well below freezing, the crushed potatoes freeze into *chuno* which is then made into flour. An alternative method involves dipping whole potatoes in water, leaving them out overnight, and then trampling the moisture out of them with bare feet (!).

Such techniques were all very well for residents of the Arctic or Andes, or for those in warmer climes rich enough to import ice from distant snowy regions. But the race was on to find a practical solution for everyone else. One promising idea was to harness the power of evaporation to conduct heat away from a receptacle of liquid. The Ancient Egyptians had made many a slave stay up all night wetting the outside of earthenware jars to cool the water within. But this approach was hard work.

The eventual answer, after a phase which was dominated by complicated devices that relied on repeatedly condensing and then evaporating gases such as ammonia, depended on the skillful use of electricity. In 1925 Clarence Birdseye unveiled his patented "Quick Freeze Machine." While working as a fur trapper in icy Labrador, he had noticed that food frozen at –40°F and below, tasted remarkably fresh when thawed. This was because the process happened so quickly that large, damaging ice crystals were unable to form. After years of working out how to duplicate such temperatures in the warmer south, he had paved the way for everyone to have an Arctic in their home.

Home freezing may seem straightforward, but there are a couple of important things to bear in mind. Firstly, the process doesn't actually kill micro-organisms, it just renders them dormant. Once the food is defrosted, they spring back into life. Secondly, great care needs to be taken with the preparation of foods for the freezer. The process must be rapid to minimise tissue damage. Full instructions are given below.

BLANCHING

Living plants contain enzymes which orchestrate their growth and maturation. When a vegetable is picked, its enzymes are still active, and unless something is done about them, they will continue to influence it. This can have adverse effects on taste, texture, and appearance. Asparagus, for example, will start to taste grassy. Its stalks will toughen and their color will fade.

Briefly immersing vegetables in boiling water or steam halts the action of their enzymes, and this is the rationale behind blanching them prior to freezing. Almost all vegetables benefit from the procedure. Here are some basic tips:

Use as large a pot of boiling water as possible—at least five and preferably 10 quarts. This will minimize the time the water ceases boiling when you add the vegetables. This helps them to retain their color.

Fill a very clean sink with ice water. Once vegetables have been blanched for the prescribed period, they need to be chilled immediately or they become faded, soft, and pulpy.

The quicker you freeze vegetables, the better. If you plan to process a large batch, turn down your freezer temperature in advance, to prepare it for the extra load. Make sure you don't overload or the vegetables will take an inordinate amount of time to freeze.

CUTTING AND PORTIONING

Whatever you are freezing, you need to think hard about how you are going to package it. The problem is that once you have frozen it, it will be very hard. As hard as ice, in fact. Unless you do a little forward planning, you will end up with a gigantic, unwieldy block of vegetables welded together with ice.

The solution is to initially freeze or part-freeze the vegetables in small, individual clusters. To do this, use the tray method:

Take the largest metal or plastic tray that will fit in your freezer and arrange the other freezer contents to make room for it. It needs to sit flat and stable and to have a little headspace.

Blanch the vegetables if appropriate, then dry them thoroughly on paper towels. If you leave their surfaces wet, they will stick to their surroundings as they freeze.

Now arrange the vegetables into small mounds on the tray, looking to be about a third-cup in volume.

Carefully transport the tray to the freezer, making sure that the piles remain intact and separate, and leave inside the freezer until frozen.

Remove the tray and transfer the individual clumps of vegetables into freezer bags. A spatula will help you separate the mounds from the trays. If they are stuck fast, run some cool water over the other side of the tray to help dislodge the portions.

Label the bags with the contents and date, and store in the freezer.

Some vegetables need to be cut (e.g., zucchini) or broken up into florets (e.g., broccoli) before you freeze them. You won't be able to do it afterwards. Recommendations for specific items are given on page 215.

USEFUL EQUIPMENT
- **A very large pot**
- **Large metal or plastic trays**
- **A long-handled "bird's nest" or large slotted spoon** (for removing vegetables from boiling water)
- **Ice**
- **Labels**
- **Paper towels**
- **Resealable freezer bags**
- **Plastic containers with tight-fitting lids** (these should be rectangular rather than round for efficient storage)

DUXELLE OF MUSHROOMS

This is a crafty way of preparing mushrooms for the freezer. A "duxelle" is simply a finely chopped vegetable (let's not get into the taxonomic status of fungi) which in this case is cooked up with garlic, shallots, and herbs. The technique works with many different kinds of mushroom; you can experiment with different mixes as well as making "single species" duxelles, for instance with chanterelles.

The other day Nick added a couple of frozen blocks of porcini/cèpe/boletus duxelle to a carbonara sauce. The outcome was, needless to say, delicious.

> ¼ cup (½ stick) unsalted butter
> 2 shallots, peeled and finely chopped
> 1 or 2 cloves of garlic, finely chopped
> 1 pound mixed mushrooms, finely chopped
>   (about 4½–5½ cups)
> Salt and pepper
> ¼ cup chicken or vegetable broth
> A sprig of parsley, chopped
> A few more herbs, if you like, such as thyme, chives,
>   or dill, chopped

Melt the butter in a pan and gently fry the shallots and garlic until softened.

Add the mushrooms and a little salt and pepper. Fry until the 'shrooms have released their juices.

Add the broth and increase the heat until it's reduced to just a very little broth left at the bottom of the pan. Finally, stir in the herbs.

Store in the fridge if you're planning to use within 24 hours, otherwise pour into ice trays and freeze. The duxelle will keep for several months once it is frozen.

CEPE AND SPINACH SALAD WITH GINGER VINAIGRETTE

Cèpes (*Boletus edulis*) are the mushroom-hunter's holy grail. Their dense, meaty flesh stands up particularly well to the freezer. Small specimens can be frozen whole. They should be cooked directly from the freezer, although you'll need to let them partially defrost if you plan to slice them.

Any frozen or for that matter fresh mushroom could be substituted for the cèpes. Serves 2

THE DRESSING
2 teaspoons honey
2 teaspoon sesame seeds, dry-fried for 2 minutes until slightly toasted
Juice of 1 lime
1 tablespoon sesame oil
1 tablespoon tamari
2 tablespoons chopped fresh ginger

THE SALAD
8 small frozen cèpes (porcini mushrooms)
1 tablespoon vegetable oil
Small knob of butter
8 ounces baby leaf spinach (about 7–8 cups), washed thoroughly
1 medium carrot, roughly grated or cut into a julienne
3 scallions, finely sliced

Place all the ingredients for the dressing in a small container with a tight-fitting lid and shake vigorously.

Remove the cèpes from the freezer. When they have slightly defrosted, cut them into quarters. Heat up the vegetable oil in a frying pan and fry the cèpes over medium to fierce heat until browned nicely on each side. Reserve.

Melt the butter in the same pan, then add the spinach and wilt it by cooking until it has halved in volume.

Mix the carrot julienne with the spinach in a large bowl, then pile the salad onto the plates and lay the cèpe quarters on top. Garnish with scallions.

Shake the dressing again, add about one tablespoon to each plate, then serve.

FREEZING INSTRUCTIONS FOR INDIVIDUAL VEGETABLES

All vegetables must be washed thoroughly before freezing, then blanched. Either plunge into a large quantity of water on a rolling boil for the time specified, or steam them for 50 percent longer.

ASPARAGUS
Only freeze tender asparagus. Trim off the stalk ends and cut into sections if you like. Blanch medium asparagus for three minutes, thick spears for slightly longer, and thin ones for slightly shorter. Cool promptly, then freeze.

BEANS (GREEN STRING BEANS AND YELLOW WAX BEANS)
Trim and slice the beans and slice if long. Blanch for three minutes.

BEETS
Boil for 40 minutes. Cool, then peel and slice before freezing.

BROCCOLI AND CAULIFLOWER
Separate into florets and blanch for three minutes before cooling. Tray freeze before packaging.

BRUSSEL SPROUTS
Trim and boil for five minutes before cooling and freezing.

CABBAGE AND CHINESE GREENS (E.G., BOK CHOY AND CHOY SUM)
Slice and blanch for two minutes before cooling and freezing.

CARROTS
Blanch them for five minutes if small and whole, or two minutes if sliced or cut into strips.

CORN ON THE COB
Blanch for nine minutes if you want to freeze them whole. Otherwise, blanch for three minutes, chill, then shave the kernels from the cobs. Bag them and freeze them.

GREENS (INCLUDING SPINACH AND SWISS CHARD)
Blanch for two minutes, then chill and drain well. You can remove most of the moisture by putting the greens in a strainer and pressing against them with a spoon.

MUSHROOMS
There are various ways of freezing mushrooms, depending on the species. See recipes for Duxelle of Mushrooms (page 213) and Cèpe and Ginger Salad (page 214).

ONIONS
Do not need to be blanched. You can just chop them and freeze them.

PEAS
Blanch shelled peas for one and a half minutes before freezing.

PEPPERS
Again, you don't need to blanch them. Just seed and chop before freezing.

ZUCCHINI
Blanch them whole for four minutes, adjusting this time if they're particularly thin or thick. Slice when cool, then freeze.

NB: All vegetables should be cooked straight from the freezer—don't defrost them before cooking.

FREEZING FRUIT

There is much to be said for using the tray method (see page 212) when freezing fruit. This will make it easier to remove the desired quantity from the bag when you want to use them.

Freezing can harm the structure of some fruits. Although this won't necessarily impair their flavor, the damage can be minimized by carrying out the freezing as quickly as possible after picking.

SUGARING

Some fruits survive better in the freezer if they are lightly sugared beforehand. This is true of blackberries, strawberries, black currants, red currants and plums. Other soft fruits, including blueberries and raspberries, freeze perfectly well as they are. If you are sugaring fruit prior to freezing, aim for a light, even coating.

In practice, Nick often cooks his fruit before freezing. With plums, for example, he will remove the pits, add a little sugar, cook until soft, then batch it up and freeze.

Fruit purees and coulis can also be frozen. To make a coulis, boil the fruit with 25 percent of its volume of sugar, then sieve.

RECIPES

Freezing is not only useful for preserving food. It is also an integral part of the preparation of some of our favorite desserts and snacks. Where would we be without ice cream? During the Second World War, the US government deemed it an "essential foodstuff" crucial to military morale. American air crews sometimes made it by hitching large cans filled with ice cream mix to their aircraft. During a sortie, the constant motion and extreme cold at altitude would do the work for them.

We're not going into the mysteries of ice cream making here, but we do provide you with recipes for two simple frozen treats. One is a dinner party item, the second more of a snack.

ELDERFLOWER SORBET WITH CHAMPAGNE

If you've ever walked through an elderflower wood in spring, you'll know that the flowers have a pretty heady aroma. You don't need many to flavor whatever concoction you're working on. A few heads are enough for this powerful yet delicate sorbet.

1 cup sugar
1 cup water
10 flowering elderflower heads
1½ cups champagne
Juice and zest of 1 lime
2 egg whites

Combine the sugar and the water in a medium-sized saucepan. Boil for five minutes, then remove from the heat and add the elderflowers. Let them infuse for one hour, then strain off the liquid and discard the elderflowers.

Add the champagne, lime juice, and zest, then freeze in a plastic container, stirring occasionally

When the sorbet is frozen but not completely hard, take it out of the freezer and cut it into rough chunks. Then blend them with the egg whites. This will take about one minute in a food processor.

Pour the mixture back into the container and immediately return to the freezer.

Take the sorbet out of the freezer 10 minutes before you plan to eat it.

Try serving in shot glasses as an elegant palate cleanser.

RIGHTEOUS RASPBERRY POPSICLES

The genius of these popsicles is that they contain no dairy products or refined sugar. You can suck on them with a clear conscience and allow your children to do the same. And neither of you should have cause for complaint. Nick made some of these popsicles from a collection of wild and albino raspberries assembled in the Pyrenees, and on the Wicklow Way in England.

12 ounces (about 2–2½ cups) raspberries
¾ cup clear honey
Juice of 1 medium lemon
Popsicle molds (available in catering shops and department stores)
Ice cream sticks*

*You can buy these in catering shops and department stores. Alternatively, use wooden kabob skewers cut to size.

Heat the raspberries in a saucepan along with the honey and lemon juice until the mixture comes to a boil. Remove from the heat and mash with a potato masher.

Put the mixture through a food mill or conical perforated sieve with a pestle to get rid of the seeds.

Let it cool, then pour into the popsicle molds. Insert the popsicle sticks, then freeze.

USEFUL ADDRESSES

The following are useful sources of advice, equipment and other supplies:

DRYING

In the UK:
www.ukjuicers.com
Sells a small selection of food dehydrators online

In the US:
www.drystore.com
US-based company selling dehydrators, vacuum-packers etc.

SMOKING

We showed you how to build both a cold- and a hot-smoker in Chapter 3, but you may prefer to buy one:

In the UK:
www.coldsmoker.com
makers of the 'West Country Cold-smoker'. Ship throughout the EC.

Gerry's of Wimbledon
170 The Broadway, London SW19 1RX
Tel: (020) 8542 7792
Suppliers of Shakespeare and Abu hot-smokers. Mail order.

In Canada and the USA:
Wells Can Company Limited
8705 Government Street, Burnaby, BC,
V3N 4G9 Canada
Tel: (604) 420 0959
www.wellscan.ca
Online vendors of the Bradley Smoker, a nifty machine capable of both cold- and hot-smoking.

SAUSAGES

In the UK:
The Natural Casing Company
High Point, Dippenhall, Farnham,
Surrey GU10 5EB
Tel: 01252 850 454
This company also sells saltpeter.

In the US:
www.butcher-packer.com
Suppliers of casings, starter cultures, curing mixes, and sausage-stuffing machines. Also smokers, thermometers, and vacuum-packing equipment.

CANNING

Home Canning Supply
PO Box 1158-WW, Ramana,
CA 92065, USA
Tel: (760) 7880520
www.homecanningsupply.com
US-based company, but ships internationally. Sells canners, dehydrators, jars, etc.

www.canningpantry.com
www.polsteins.com
www.homesteadharvest.com
These three companies all sell canning equipment but do not currently ship outside North America.

SUGAR—JAM-MAKING EQUIPMENT

In the UK:
Wares of Knutsford
36a Princess Street, Knutsford, Cheshire
www.waresofknutsford.co.uk
Online vendors of jam jars, funnels, straining bags, etc.

In the US:
www.kitchenkrafts.com
Sell a wide range of jam-making, home-canning, and other preserving equipment.

FERMENTING

Koji starter culture for making miso (page 148) is available online and shipped internationally from:

G.E.M. Cultures
30301 Sherwood Road, Fort Bragg,
CA 95437, USA
Tel: (707) 9642922
www.gemcultures.com

AIR EXCLUSION—VACUUM SEALERS

www.kitchenkrafts.com
They will ship worldwide.

In the US:
www.butcher-packer.com
www.drystore.com
www.homesteadharvest.com

MISCELLANEOUS

The UK-based firm Wild Harvest are friends of ours who supply game and other high-quality meats as well as first-rate wild mushrooms. They have an efficient home-delivery service.

Wild Harvest Ltd
Units B61–4 New Covent Garden
Market, London SW8 5HH
Tel: (020) 7498 5397
www.wildharvestuk.com

INDEX

To Amy Mei

Many people have helped or inspired us in the writing of this book. In particular, we'd like to thank: Hugh Fearnley-Whittingstall for his generous foreword, Janie Suthering for her helpful suggestions and advice, The Women's Institute and the National Trust for pickling tips, Simon Benning, James Harder, Valentino, and Maria Rosa for help with sausages, Justin Percival for directions to an inexhaustible supply of sloes, and Hazel Holt for her microbial knowledge. We must also thank Keiko (sugar), Nigel (figs), Camilla (plums), Jane (paté), David (biltong), and Penelope (quinces) for help with specific items. Muna Reyal has been an endlessly patient and good-humored editor, Carl Hodson has done a great design job and Peter Cassidy has produced some truly wonderful photography, aided by Linda Tubby's brilliant interpretations of the recipes.

This edition published in 2004 by Kyle Books, an imprint of Kyle Cathie Limited.
www.kylecathie.com

Distributed by National Book Network
4501 Forbes Blvd., Suite 200, Lanham, MD 20706
Phone: (301) 459 3366   Fax: (301) 429 5746

This paperback published in 2009

ISBN: 978-1-906868-02-4

Nick Sandler and Johnny Acton are hereby identified as the authors of this work in accordance with Section 77 of the Copyright, Designs and Patents Act 1988.

Text © 2004 Nick Sandler and Johnny Acton
Photography © 2004 Peter Cassidy
Book design © 2004 Kyle Cathie Limited

Senior Editor Muna Reyal
Designer Carl Hodson
Photographer Peter Cassidy
Food stylist for the recipe photography Linda Tubby
Styling Wei Tang
Editorial assistant Jennifer Wheatley
Production Sha Huxtable and Alice Holloway

The Library of Congress Cataloguing-in-Publication Data is available on file.

Color reproduction by Sang Choy
Printed and bound in Singapore by Tien-Wah Press